Standards and Curriculum: A View from the Nation

A Joint Report by the
National Council of Teachers of Mathematics (NCTM)
and the
Association of State Supervisors of Mathematics (ASSM)

Park City, Utah
July 21–24, 2004

Edited by
Johnny W. Lott, Past President, NCTM
Kathleen Nishimura, Past President, ASSM

NATIONAL COUNCIL OF
TEACHERS OF MATHEMATICS

Library of Congress Cataloging-in-Publication Data

Standards and curriculum : a view from the nation, a joint report by the National Council of
Mathematics (NCTM) and the Association of State Supervisors of Mathematics (ASSM), Park
City, Utah, July 21-24, 2004 / edited by Johnny W. Lott, Kathleen Nishimura.
          p. cm.
      Includes bibliographical references.
      ISBN 0-87353-581-2
1. Mathematics—Study and teaching (Secondary)—Standards—United States—Congresses.
2. Mathematics—Study and teaching (Higher)—Standards—United States—Congresses.
3. Education, Secondary—Curricula—United States—Congresses. 4. Education, Higher—
Curricula—United States—Congresses I. Lott, Johnny W., 1944- II. Nishimura, Kathleen.
III. National Council of Teachers of Mathematics. IV. Association of State Supervisors of
Mathematics.
      QA13.S68 2004
      510'.71'073—dc22

                          2005002750

The National Council of Teachers of Mathematics is a public voice of mathematics
education, providing vision, leadership, and professional development to support teachers in
ensuring mathematics learning of the highest quality for all students.

The publications of the National Council of Teachers of Mathematics present a variety of
viewpoints. The views expressed or implied in this publication, unless otherwise noted, should
not be interpreted as official positions of the Council.

This material is based on work supported by the National Science Foundation under
Grant No. ESI-0408562. Any opinions, findings, and conclusions or recommendations expressed
in this material are those of the author(s) and do not necessarily reflect the views of the National
Science Foundation.

Printed in the United States of America

Contents

Foreword --- vii
      Cathy Seeley
      President, National Council of Teachers of Mathematics
      Wesley Bird
      President, Association of State Supervisors of Mathematics

Acknowledgments --- ix

Introduction: Setting the Stage for the Comparison of Mathematics Standards: A Joint Proposal ------------------------- 1
      Johnny W. Lott
      University of Montana, Missoula, Montana

Mathematics Standards: A Grade-Level Comparison
1.   **Kindergarten: Process and Standards** ------------------------------- 7
      Trecina H. Green, Chair; *Mississippi Department of Education*
      Herb Clemens, *Director, Park City Mathematics Institute*
      Kathleen Nishimura, Codirector, *National Math View;*
              Hawaii State Department of Education
      Michael Roach, *Indiana Department of Education*
      Cathy Seeley, *National Council of Teachers of Mathematics*

2.   **Grade 1: Process and Standards** -------------------------------------- 9
      Bonnie Hagelberger, Chair; *Plymouth, Minnesota*
      Toni Meyer, *North Carolina Department of Public Instruction*
      Barbara Montalto, *Austin, Texas*
      Sue White, *Washington, D.C., School District*

3.   **Grade 2: Process and Standards** -------------------------------------- 13
      Sally Caldwell, Chair; *Delaware Department of Education*
      Kaye Forgione, *Achieve, Inc., Austin, Texas*
      Diana Kasbaum, *Wisconsin Department of Public Instruction*
      Mari Muri, *Cromwell, Connecticut*
      Mattye Pollard-Cole, *Centennial, Colorado*
      Mary Ruzga, *South Carolina State Department of Education*

4.   Grade 3: Process and Standards --- 17

David DeCoste, Chair; *Saint Xavier College, Nova Scotia*
Claudia Ahlstrom, *New Mexico Public Education Department*
Susan Iida, *Sacramento, California*
Anne M. Mikesell, *Ohio Department of Education*

5.   Grade 4: Process and Standards --- 21

Jeane Joyner, Chair; *Raleigh, North Carolina*
Gail Englert, *School of International Studies at Meadowbrook,*
                    Norfolk, Virginia
Bob Robinson, *Everett, Washington*
Diane L. Schaefer, *Rhode Island Department of Education*

6.   Grade 5: Process and Standards --- 25

Cindy Bryant, Chair; *Salem, Missouri*
Wesley Bird, *Missouri Department of Education*
Glenn Bruckhart, *Littleton, Colorado*
Robert Kansky, *Cheyenne, Wyoming*
Harvey Keynes, *University of Minnesota*
Barbara Stewart, *Conesus, New York*

7.   Grade 6: Process and Standards --- 29

Barbara Reys, Chair; *University of Missouri—Columbia*
Carolyn Baldree, *Georgia Department of Education*
Donna Taylor, *North Carolina Department of Public Instruction*
Stephen Wilson, *Johns Hopkins University*

8.   Grade 7: Process and Standards --- 33

Jennie Bennett, Chair; *Houston, Texas*
Judith Keeley, *Rhode Island Department of Education*
Andy Magid, *University of Oklahoma*
Sarah F. Mason, *Alabama Department of Education*
Paula Moeller, *Texas Education Agency*
Carolyn Sessions, *Louisiana Department of Education*

9.   Grade 8: Process and Standards --- 37

Laurie Boswell, Chair; *Monroe, New Hampshire*
Jerry Dancis, *University of Maryland*
Dan Hupp, *Maine Department of Education*
Michael Kestner, *U.S. Department of Education*

Frank Marburger, *Pennsylvania Department of Education*
Lois Williams, *Virginia Department of Education*

10. Grade 9: Process and Standards—Algebra ----------------------- 41
Rick Jennings, Chair; *Washington State Office of the
    Department of Public Instruction*
Ann Bartosh, *Kentucky Department of Education*
Daniel Dolan, *Cromwell, Connecticut*
Linda Hackett, *Department of Education Agency*
Roger Howe, *Yale University*
Anthony Scott, *Chicago, Illinois*

11. Grade 10: Process and Standards—Geometry -------------------- 45
Richard Seitz, Chair; *Helena, Montana*
Deborah Bliss, *Virginia Department of Education*
Margaret Bondorew, *Foxboro, Massachusetts*
Scott Eddins, *Tennessee Department of Education*
Jerry Evans, *Utah Department of Education*
William McCallum, *University of Arizona*

12. Grade 11: Process and Standards—Algebra II, Precalculus ---- 49
M. Kathleen Heid, Chair; *Penn State University*
David Brancamp, *Nevada Department of Education*
Jerry Dwyer, *Texas Tech University*
David Hoff, *Bottineau, North Dakota*
James Rubillo, *National Council of Teachers of Mathematics*

**13. Grade 12: Process and Standards—Grades 9–12,
Probability and Statistics** --- 55
Michael Koehler, Chair; *Kansas City, Missouri*
Martha Aliaga, *American Statistical Association*
Tracy Newell, *Kansas State Department of Education*
Frank Quinn, *Virginia Polytechnic Institute*
Robert Riehs, *New Jersey Department of Education*

Limitations of the Study --- 61

Contents

Conclusions --- 63

References --- 67

Appendix I: Participants --- 69

**Appendix II: Summary of State Mathematics
        Grade Level Documents** -- 71

Appendix III: Example of Original Template --------------------------- 89

Appendix IV: Example of Adapted Template --------------------------- 97

Appendix V: Standards with Less Agreement -------------------------- 119

NATIONAL COUNCIL OF TEACHERS OF MATHEMATICS

December 20, 2004

The United States is one of the few countries in the world without a national curriculum. Each state, and sometimes each district or school, can identify its own expectations for what mathematics students should know or be able to do. This joint project between NCTM and ASSM provides insights into where we may be headed as a nation in terms of our expectations for students' mathematics learning. The report lays a foundation for discussions about the future direction of local, state, and national mathematics curricula.

This collaborative effort among mathematics educators, state mathematics supervisors, and mathematicians has provided far more than the written results included in this report. Perhaps even more important than these findings are the constructive discussions among these constituencies and the groundwork laid for future work together toward a high-quality mathematics education for every student.

I encourage you to use this report to stimulate discussion in your own community. More than that, I encourage you to be part of the broader discussion(s) that need to take place over the next several years around questions like these:

- Who should be involved in making curriculum decisions for students?
- What should be the role of schools, school districts, states, and the federal government on defining mathematics expectations?
- How much attention should we pay to what is done in other states' mathematics standards?

Most of all, I encourage you to experience for yourselves the power of constructive discussions and collaboration among mathematics educators, mathematicians, policymakers, and the public toward improving the mathematics learning of every student in this nation.

Sincerely,

Cathy Seeley
President
National Council of Teachers of Mathematics

ASSOCIATION of STATE SUPERVISORS of MATHEMATICS

President
Wesley L. Bird
Missouri Department of Education
P. O. Box 480
Jefferson City, MO 65102-0480
Wesley.Bird@dese.mo.gov

1st Vice President
Paula Moeller
Texas Education Agency
1701 N. Congress Avenue
Austin, TX 78701
512-463-9588
pmoeller@tea.state.tx.us

2nd Vice President
Jerry L. Evans
Utah Department of Education
P. O. Box 144200
Salt Lake City, UT 84114-4200
jevans@usoe.k12.ut.us

3rd Vice President
Deborah K. Bliss
Virginia Department of Education
P. O. Box 2120
Richmond, VA 23218-2120
804-786-6418
dbliss@mail.vak12ed.edu

Secretary
Carolyn L. Baldree
Georgia Department of Education
1754 Twin Towers East
Atlanta, GA 30334-5040
cbaldree@doe.k12.ga.us

Financial Officer
Charles D. Watson
Arkansas Department of Education
#4 State Capitol Mall
Little Rock, AR 72201
cwatson@arkedu.k12.ar.us

Past President
Kathleen Nishimura
OCISS-ISB
475 22nd Avenue
Building 302, Room 116
Honolulu, HI 96816
808-733-9141 ext. 414
Kathleen_Nishimura/OIS/HIDOE
@notes.k12.hi.us

In 2000, the publication of *Principles and Standards for School Mathematics* became a major milestone for the mathematics community by providing and modeling current research and effective instructional practices in mathematics education. Educational institutions at the state and local levels used *Principles and Standards* as a springboard for revising their mathematics curricula. This report, *Standards and Curriculum: A View from the Nation* provides a snapshot of how state agencies viewed and constructed mathematical standards to both support curriculum reform and serve as a blueprint for future testing under the No Child Left Behind Act (2001).

The publication of *Standards and Curriculum* is an initial attempt to examine across states the impact of *Principles and Standards* on curriculum reform, discern how state educational agencies approached the task of developing state standards, and bring to light areas of commonality and difference. Of considerable interest are the varying degrees of specificity of state mathematics standards but at the same time evidence of the existence of overarching threads that support the "big ideas" of mathematics.

Members of the Association of State Supervisors of Mathematics (ASSM) play a vital role in helping steer the direction of mathematics education at the state level. The information obtained from the *Standards and Curriculum* endeavor will be used by mathematics supervisors to further evaluate and refine state initiatives. The stage is now set for future dialogue concerning the direction of mathematics reform and the sharing of ideas among national, state, and local educational agencies. The development of rigorous state standards for all students is a daunting task but essential for empowering and creating productive citizens. The data produced as a result of the *Standards and Curriculum* project will serve as a foundation for future initiatives revolving around mathematics standards.

Wesley Bird
President, ASSM

Acknowledgments

We want to acknowledge the support and participation of the boards of directors of the National Council of Teachers of Mathematics and the Association of State Supervisors of Mathematics for agreeing to meet and hold meetings in Park City, Utah, in conjunction with the work of the National Math View Project. In addition, we want to acknowledge the support and help of Herb Clemens, director, and the staff of the Park City Mathematics Institute (PCMI) in making the participants feel welcome and incorporating the participants into a part of the regular activities of PCMI.

Without the assistance and funding of the National Science Foundation, this work would not have been possible. In particular, we need to thank Dr. John Bradley for his help with grant details.

We also want to thank other contributors to the report, who include the following:

Hyman Bass, *University of Michigan*

Robert Kenney, *Burlington, Vermont*

Kathy Mowers, President-Elect, American Mathematical Association of Two-Year Colleges; *Owensboro Community and Technical College*

Nanci Spears, *Juneau, Alaska*

Johnny W. Lott
Kathleen Nishimura
Codirectors, National Math View Project

Board of Directors
National Council of Teachers of Mathematics

Board of Directors
Association of State Supervisors of Mathematics

Introduction

Setting the Stage for the Comparison of Mathematics Standards:
A Joint Proposal

Johnny W. Lott, University of Montana

The movement for standards in mathematics taught in grades K–12 began in earnest with the publication of the 1989 *Curriculum and Evaluation Standards for School Mathematics* (NCTM) and rapidly continued with the publishing of individual state standards. In 2003, all states except Iowa had published state standards for mathematics (CCSSO 2003). With its *Principles and Standards for School Mathematics* (2000), the National Council of Teachers of Mathematics (NCTM) showed that standards can and should be revised over time to meet the needs of the community at large. Similarly, states across the nation have begun revising standards for mathematics, and this type of work is expected to continue for some time.

The movement to develop state standards has continued, and it appears that the United States has come closer than ever before to having a de facto national curriculum. This national movement has happened in spite of U.S. constitutional guarantees that the issue of schools and curricular issues are in the state domain as opposed to the federal domain.

Concerns over standards have developed from the reports of the Third International Mathematics and Science Study (TIMSS) and the reports growing out of the work of Schmidt (2003) and Stigler and Hiebert (1997). Schmidt reported that the mathematics curriculum across the United States was a mile wide and an inch deep when compared with the national curricula of many higher scoring countries around the world.

In another report, Raimi and Braden (1998) "ranked state standards" on a scale from 1 to 16, giving states marks on aspects including content and clarity. In most of the work to date, the conclusions are based on textbooks used and not necessarily the standards themselves (Schmidt, 2003; Schmidt, McKnight, and Raizen 1997). Many of the conclusions are based on comparing content of instruction with scores on tests, which may be reasonable because most believe that students are more likely to learn the content that they are taught. There is an implicit (and sometimes explicit) assumption that the texts determine the content of what is taught. This assumption might or might not be true depending on whether teachers teach what is in textbooks. In today's world, it may be the case that more and more teachers are teaching toward what is tested (Floden et al. 1981). Also today, what is tested is primarily determined by the state standards or grade-level expectations growing out of those standards.

With the current and previous presidential administrations, the United States Department of Education has pushed for a national eighth-grade mathematics test and then settled for a set of state tests to be implemented in the near future for Grades 3–8. These federal initiatives have been tied to money for education flowing from the federal level to the states. Thus, there has been a move to consider a level of tests that could be used for national or federal purposes with no apparent national curriculum in place on which to base the tests (U.S. Department of Education, www.ed.gov/nclb/accountability/ayp/testingforresults.html). As states move into testing, using individual sets of standards as required in the No Child Left Behind Act (2001), knowing how consistent the standards are across state lines and from a national perspective is very important.

It has become increasingly important for the NCTM and the Association of State Supervisors of Mathematics (ASSM) to help teachers across the nation prepare students for mandated tests in the absence of a stated national curriculum. So important is this issue that discussion begun in 2002–2003 led to a consideration of whether a de facto national curriculum is being used. If indeed such a curriculum is being used, expecting that state instruments may be meshed to frame a truly national assessment is reasonable. If in fact significant disparities exist in the various state curricula, commonality of norms and national assessment become more problematic.

To determine similarities and differences in state standards that direct curriculum, NCTM and ASSM proposed a grant, *A National Mathematics View*, to the National Science Foundation (NSF) to allow the set of state supervisors (or in the absence of a state supervisor of mathematics, an official of state education department) to come together with a small number of NCTM members and a set of mathematicians and statisticians to compare the standards from a national perspective.

The Joint Proposal

In May 2004, NSF funded the proposal and work began on convening the state supervisors (members of ASSM) with a group of mathematicians and mathematics educators from NCTM. An arrangement was made with the Park City Mathematics Institute (PCMI) to have the work sessions in Park City, Utah. This site was chosen because PCMI conducts study sessions for mathematicians, mathematics teachers, international mathematics educators, researchers, graduate students, and undergraduate students in both mathematics and mathematics education. With its ties to the Institute for Advanced Study, located in Princeton, New Jersey, and with Park City being the "writing home" of NCTM's *Standards* (1989), it was a perfect backdrop to consider major issues of mathematics education in a setting with both mathematics educators and mathematicians.

Participants

The National Mathematics View codirectors, Johnny W. Lott and Kathleen Nishimura, assembled 74 individuals to do the work of considering standards. The group included the following:

- Forty-seven people who were either state supervisors, members of the Board of Directors of ASSM, representatives of states, or knowledgeable members of the community who were well acquainted with state standards; standards of Washington, D.C.; or standards of American international schools
- Twelve individuals who were either mathematicians or statisticians and who had been identified as having a leadership role in the Mathematics Association of America (MAA), the American Mathematics Society (AMS), the American Statistical Association (ASA), or the American Association of Two-Year Colleges (AMATYC) or as one who would participate in a companion grant funded by NSF to Dr. Roger Howe of PCMI; or who represented other mathematics education groups. (Dr. Howe's grant was designed to consider state standards and make recommendations about them from a purely mathematical point of view as to structure, coherence, and comprehensiveness. [It is noted that one individual declined at the last minute because of a death in the family.])
- NCTM's Executive Director and 14 mathematics educators identified by NCTM who were members of its Board of Directors

For the chore of comparing state standards, the participants were divided into groups that included 3 to 4 members of the state supervisor group above, one of the mathematicians from group two above, and 1 to 2 from the last group. The groups are listed with the individual sections of this report and in Appendix I.

Standards to Be Compared

ASSM members were asked to submit the most recent state standards and any supporting documentation that might be helpful in considering the standards. With those submitted, the near complete set of standards of all states available from the Council of Chief State School Officers (2003) and from the Center for the Study of Mathematics Curriculum at the University of Missouri in Columbia gathered by Mr. Shannon Dingman under the direction of Dr. Barbara Reys, the mathematics standards from all states except Iowa were collected. (Iowa does not have official state standards.) The principal rule followed in the collecting of standards was that they had to be the most recent ones that had been "approved" at the state level. Supporting documents included the grade-level expectations that are being required by the U. S. Department of Education as a part of the No Child Left Behind Act. A listing of what was available for the work, a listing of dates for those documents, and a view of how rapidly the scene is changing can be found in Appendix II.

Process of Comparing Standards

Several models are available to guide the work of looking for commonalities and differences in the complete sets of state standards at grade level. Work by Blank (2003) on the enacted mathematics curriculum. was developed around 11 states and coded the "most important" concepts in the curriculum. This work provided an initial framework considered for the analysis of state standards based on the work of Andrew Porter (2002). Webb (1999) has also worked on an analysis process.

Porter's work is the first to be considered in guiding the comparison of the state standards. In "Measuring the Content of Instruction: Uses in Research and Practice," Porter described tools for measuring the content of instruction, the content of instructional materials, and the alignment between these (Porter 2002). The tools described consider topics versus cognitive demands and are used by Blank, Porter, and Smithson (2001) in developing topographical pictures of individual states. However, in interviews with Porter when the proposal was being submitted (October 2003) and shortly after the proposal was funded (June 2004), he discussed the use and validity of his tools for comparing standards. He suggested that mathematics education "experts" (such as members of NCTM and ASSM) could be trained to use the tools in a very short time. In the discussion of the cognitive demands, Porter explained that when the tool was being used with state standards, trained experts had no trouble deciding whether a standard subpart fit into a particular cognitive demand. However, further discussion revealed that if the model were used with all states, its application would take approximately three times the amount of time that was allotted for the project. For this primary reason, the method was not used. Time simply did not allow its use.

The model that was adopted (and adapted) for use with the project was developed for use with the Second International Mathematics Study (SIMS) (Bulletin IV, IEA 1979). As noted by Hirstein in conference proceedings (1980) and in a private conversation (June 2004), the method was used because it was "recognized that the level of formalism regarding a national curriculum varies; in some countries there is a national mathematics syllabus while other exercise little formal control over the content offered by individual schools." Hirstein's description of the international survey of national curricula from around the globe was very similar to the level of state standards in the United States in 2004. Further investigation showed that a set of topics was pre-identified, and each country then was coded with a *0* to indicate that a topic was not taught in the country or with a + to indicate that the topic was taught.

To use a model similar to the one described by Hirstein (1980), participants would need a recording sheet for the standards that was adaptable to the many forms of standards seen in different states. After much consideration, an advisory committee comprised of members of ASSM and NCTM recommended that a template model be adopted. To construct the template model for a grade, each state was examined and standards that appeared to be listed on several states were incorporated into a "grade level" template. The template was intended neither to be a complete picture nor to pre-empt the work that was to come; it was simply designed to list standards at grade level. An example of the initial template developed for the fifth-grade set of standards is presented in Appendix III.

The template of Appendix III was tried with one strand: the number and operations strand. After that was tried, it became clear that participants either would need a wider range of standards listed or would need to add many standards to the list to have a comprehensive comparison across all sets of standards. Because of this, the advisory committee recommended that, to consider a set of standards for a given grade level, participants would receive the standards for the preceding and succeeding grades. The preceding set of standards was presented in italic type on a large chart accompanied by the grade level to be examined in bold type and the succeeding set of grade standards in regular type. An example of the modified form of the template for Grade 5 standards is given in Appendix IV.

With this model template format, coding was done in a manner similar to that used in the SIMS model. The coding used the following adapted coding of the SIMS model:

0   All members of a group agree that a standard is not present in a state.

*   Members of the group cannot agree about whether a standard is present (This primarily occurs when there is misunderstanding about the language of a standard). A standard receiving this symbol required a conference in which the following happened: If all felt that the state standard was unique (meaning probably occurring in only one state), then the standard was coded with *0. If the group agreed that it was very likely the standard would occur in at least 4 other states, then it was coded with a *1. If no agreement could be reached at all, the standard was coded with the * and the vote of the members of the group; for example, *2/3 meant that the group did not agree and was split 2 in favor and 3 opposed.

1   All members of the group agree that a standard is present in a state.

With the use of the system, in its simplest form, one can count the number of 1s in a spreadsheet with a given standard to determine how many states agree on that standard at the particular grade level. For this system to work, the reader must understand how many states were considered at the grade level.

One primary advantage of the method is that it required a very brief training period and was relatively simple to use. It does not, however, provide the wealth of information that the Porter system does. Also, this method is somewhat open to interpretation, as will be noted in the "Limitations" section of this report.

With the described coding system, each group identified the commonalities and differences at a particular grade level. In this way, a snapshot of the mathematics concepts expected in the mathematics standards in the United States was developed by grade level. Through this work, a complete picture of the mathematics suggested in state standards of 2004 emerges.

Timeline for the Work

The participants traveled to Park City, Utah, outside Salt Lake City on Wednesday, July 21. On the evening of the 21st, participants had a working dinner meeting at which they were given an overview of the work at hand were assigned to groups, and plans were set for the morning meeting July 22. Each identified group was given a complete set of state standards from 49 states, the District of Columbia, and the Department of Defense Schools. Also in the morning session, each group was given a chart with a template of standards that had been gleaned from the complete list of 51. The template was described as an aid to the work at hand. The template was not intended to be *the* set of standards that were to be checked against all states, but it provided a starting place. Groups were encouraged to cross out standards on the template that were not appropriate and to add ones that should be there. The template was used as a recording sheet to code standards. The format of the sheet is seen in Table 1.

Table 1. Coding Sheet for Standards

		AL	AK	AZ	AR	CA	CO	CT	⋯
Strand									
Number/Number Sense									
	Use place value to read and write whole numbers up to X (5–9 digits)								
	Identify place value to Xth place to Y thousands								
	Read and write numbers from Xth place to Y thousands								

Table 1 contains strands of mathematics in the leftmost column, with subparts of that strand in the next column to the right and then columns for each state to the right of that. Coding was done in the cells with state headings. In some cells, to identify places, for example the Xth place, group members were asked either to record the value of X in the cell under a state or to write the value on a Post-it® note and stick it to the recording sheet. Each recording sheet contained a template of standards at the grade level being considered, the previous grade level, and the succeeding grade level so that group members did not have to write any more new standards than absolutely necessary.

Training with the use of the coding tool was conducted on the morning of July 22 with work on comparing standards by each group taking place on July 22–24. All work was completed by 6:00 P.M. on July 24.

Reliability Check

To have a simple check on the reliability within a group doing coding at a grade level, a single section of 16 standards were chosen, and each member of the group coded each standard. Checks were then used to determine the amount of agreement among the coders. Those checks are recorded in each grade-level section.

Use of Verbs in Standards
One of the essential issues in coding standards was the interpretation of the words within the standards. The most problematic of the words is the verbs. Many states use verbs to indicate whether a standard is at the introduction stage, at the developmental stage, or at the mastery stage. Little consistency exists among the states on these verbs. Included in the lists that follow are verbs about which there was agreement. When no verbs are given, either (1) there was no agreement, or (2) states listed the topics without verbs.

1

Kindergarten: Process and Standards

Trecina H. Green, Chair; *Mississippi Department of Education*
Herb Clemens, *Director, Park City Mathematics Institute*
Kathleen Nishimura, *Codirector, National Math View; Hawaii State Department of Education*
Michael Roach, *Indiana Department of Education*
Cathy Seeley, *National Council of Teachers of Mathematics*

Process
The kindergarten team coded one state at a time as an entire group. They completed about 90 percent of the states and then revised the template to fit the states. All members of the group discussed every standard.

Reader Reliability
The reader reliability rating for the kindergarten team showed agreement on 14 out of 16 items tested (88%).

Trends in Kindergarten Standards
The kindergarten team found many different levels of standards for kindergarten. There are potentially many reasons for this, stemming from the fact that some states require all-day kindergarten while others require only half-day kindergarten for all children.

Comparison of Kindergarten Standards
The kindergarten team studied the standards for all states and selected 37 states that had enough documentation to support comparisons. When the analysis of the standards was being completed, there was a fairly clear demarcation in the standards. The dividing line appeared to be when 25 percent or more of the 37 states agreed on a particular standard. As a result, the kindergarten standards are separated into 2 groups: (1) those for which more than one-fourth of the states examined included the standard, and (2) those for which less than one-fourth of the states included the standard. As with all later grades, group (1) is included in the text and group (2) is included in Appendix V.

There are notes on some standards, particularly with regard to the Number strand, where the level varied by state. Only those with much variability are listed here. In the collation of the standards, the strands are listed in bold. The subparts are either substandards under the strand or, in some cases, grade-level expectations for the kindergarten students.

The set of standards for which at least 25 percent of the 37 states agreed follows:

Number
Count to X (where X varies from 10 to 100) (32) 86%
Represent a number in different ways: number, numeral, picture, object (28) 76%
One-to-one correspondence (26) 70%
Compare sets (more than, less than, equal to) (25) 68%

Use ordinal numbers to identify position (21) 57%
Count backward (19) 51%
Read/write whole numbers (not words) (18) 49%
Estimate number of objects (might also verify) (15) 41%
Represent whole numbers using models (e.g., place value or other models) (14) 38%
Identify next number and previous number (12) 32%
Sequence numbers (12) 32%
Compare whole numbers (greater than, less than, equal to) (11) 30%
Compose and decompose numbers (11) 30%

Operations

Model addition and subtraction with models (30) 81%
Share a whole or a set into equal parts (10) 27%

Measurement

Compare objects by measurement attributes (longer/shorter, heavier/lighter, holds more/less, etc.) (33) 89%
Recognize and name coins (pennies, nickels, dimes, and notes) (28) 76%
Measure with nonstandard units (23) 62%
Use basic time vocabulary (19) 51%
Name days of the week (13) 35%
Order events in a day (13) 35%
Compare temperatures (hotter/colder) (11) 30%
Read calendar (days, weeks, months) (11) 30%
Compare and order objects by size (10) 27%

Geometry

Identify and describe 2-dimensional shapes (32) 86%
Compare and sort figures based on attributes (i.e., color, shape; includes statements listed under algebra) (32) 86%
Use positional words (below/above, inside/outside, etc.) (29) 78%
Identify 2- and 3-dimensional objects in the real world (17) 46%
Identify 3-dimensional objects (16) 43%
Draw 2-dimensional shapes (13) 35%
Combine shapes to create 2-dimensional figures (11) 30%
Sort objects and shapes using manipulatives (10) 27%

Probability and Data Analysis

Represent data (24) 65%
Organize data (22) 59%
Collect data (20) 54%
Analyze and describe results of data collection (17) 46%
Answer questions and solve problems using graphs (15) 41%
Use physical objects to build graphs (12) 32%

Algebra (including Patterns and Functions)

Identify, recognize, and extend patterns (34) 92%
Create patterns (18) 49%
Describe patterns (including finding rule/generalization) (18) 49%
Replicate patterns (15) 41%

Problem Solving and Mathematical Processes

Solve story problems using objects and pictures (19) 51%
Use problem-solving strategies/problem-solving model (12) 32%

2

Grade 1: Process and Standards

Bonnie Hagelberger, Chair; *Plymouth, Minnesota*
Toni Meyer, *North Carolina Department of Public Instruction*
Barbara Montalto, *Austin, Texas*
Sue White, *Washington, D.C., School District*

Process

The Grade 1 team followed the suggested coding process in the introduction. Each state statement was discussed by the entire group. All recording was done on the template provided. As questions arose during the process, they were recorded on Post-it® notes and placed on the template. After the last state standard was reviewed, all Post-it® notes were re-examined; either the standards were added to the template with the appropriate states recorded or the standards were discarded.

Reader Reliability

The reader reliability rating for the Grade 1 team showed agreement on 14 out of 16 items tested (88%). According to the group, there were very few items on which they did not come to immediate agreement. A vote was needed on only 1 item during the entire process.

Trends in First-Grade Standards

As might be expected, much of the work in Grade 1 deals with numbers and number operations. This work provides the numerical basis for the mathematics that is to come. Also, beginning concepts of algebraic thinking, geometry, and data analysis are introduced.

Comparison of First-Grade Standards

The set of standards for which at least 25 percent of the 38 states agreed follows:

Number

    Compare whole numbers (greater, less, equal to); describe the difference (29) 76%

    Represent place value to 99 (29) 76%

    Skip count by 2s, 5s, and 10s (25s) (28) 74%

    Count forward to 100; read and write (27) 71%

    Model halves, thirds, fourths of a unit (27) 71%

    Different representations of whole numbers up to 100 (24) 63%

    Identify ordinal position up to tenth (20) 53%

    Count backward from 100 (18) 47%

    Sequential relationships among whole numbers (ordering whole numbers) (16) 42%

    Record and write number words to X (15) 39%

    Locate numbers on a positive number line (ordering) (14) 37%

    Estimate the size of groups (14) 37%

    Identify 1 more, 1 less, 10 more, 10 less (12) 32%

    Use expanded notation (in words) (11) 29%

Number Operations
> Add whole numbers up to 10 (or 20) (or 18) (34) 89%
> Subtract whole numbers up to 10 (26) 68%
> Use symbols "+," "-," and "=" (22) 58%
> Demonstrate meaning of addition and subtraction with manipulatives (18) 47%
> Reasonableness of answers (13) 34%
> Compose and decompose numbers (12) 32%
> Use fact families (11) 29%
> Add 3 one-digit numbers (10) 26%

Measurement
> Tell time (hour and half hour) (34) 89%
> Measure with nonstandard units (31) 82%
> Determine monetary value of coins (28) 74%
> Attributes to describe and compare objects (24) 63%
> Tell time (hour and half hour) using analog clocks (22) 58%
> Tell time (hour and half hour) using digital clocks (21) 55%
> Recognize and name penny, nickel, and dime (20) 53%
> Measure with standard units (length, weight, temperature) (16) 42%
> Estimate measurement of an object (14) 37%
> Select the most appropriate tool to measure an attribute (13) 34%
> Order according to an attribute (12) 32%

Geometry
> Identify basic shapes in 2-dimension and 3-dimension (26) 68%
> Compare figures based on characteristics (21) 55%
> Describe location of objects (20) 53%
> Sort and describe geometric objects (17) 45%
> Build/draw common 2- and 3-dimensional figures (16) 42%
> Recognize line of symmetry (15) 39%
> Use flips, slides, and turns (14) 37%
> Describe spatial relationships (i.e., inside/outside) (11) 29%
> Combine or take apart shapes to create 2-dimensional objects, shapes (10) 26%
> Describe attributes of different shapes: circle, triangle, quadrilaterals (10) 26%

Probability
> Determine least likely, most likely, and equally likely (14) 37%
> Identify probability as certain, impossible, or probable (10) 26%

Data Analysis
> Create a pictograph/picture graph (28) 74%
> Create a tally chart/table (22) 58%
> Draw bar graphs (20) 53%
> Collect data using surveys (19) 50%
> Interpret data and draw a conclusion (16) 42%
> Organize and display data (12) 32%

Algebra
> Concept of pattern—repeating (24) 63%
> Recognize, describe, and extend patterns (24) 63%
> Concept of pattern (20) 53%

Commutative property (18) 47%
Know inverse operations of addition and subtraction (17) 45%
Classify and sort objects (16) 42%
Sort objects based on attributes (15) 39%
Translate among representations of patterns (14) 37%
Create patterns using a variety of materials/objects (13) 34%
Equality (12) 32%
Identify property (12) 32%
Use missing addends (12) 32%
Identify, extend patterns in the hundreds chart (12) 32%

Problem Solving

Uses strategies for problem solving (23) 61%
Formulate problems from everyday situations (14) 37%
Solve problems (10) 26%

Reasoning

Compare information (17) 45%

Communications

 Use mathematical language (22) 58%

3

Grade 2: Process and Standards

Sally Caldwell, Chair; *Delaware Department of Education*
Kaye Forgione, *Achieve, Inc., Austin, Texas*
Diana Kasbaum, *Wisconsin Department of Public Instruction*
Mari Muri, *Cromwell, Connecticut*
Mattye Pollard-Cole, *Centennial, Colorado*
Mary Ruzga, *South Carolina State Department of Education*

Process
The Grade 2 team functioned as a collaborative group during the review of each state's standards. The state folders were evenly divided among 5 of the 6 team members. One member was the recorder for all states and standards. According to the group, having a single recorder for the entire study helped with consistency in the recording process.

For each content strand, the team reviewed standards on the given template and then considered state standards to determine if the template contained all those needed. If it did not, a list was made of the needed standards and they were categorized into groups for the specific strands. After a whole group discussion, the template was adjusted to contain needed items. An example is seen in the Number strand where under "number operations," the group determined the subcategories of "objects and manipulatives," "mental mathematics," "estimation," "technology," "paper and pencil or algorithm use," "composing and decomposing," and "invented algorithms" were needed.

After the template was adjusted, a state-by-state review of content strands was conducted as follows:
- One team member read a state standard and indicated which boxes should be checked on the template. If there were disagreements or if the standard was unclear, there was a group discussion. Consensus was reached before the item was coded.
- To test the process, the Grade 2 team worked through all standards in the data/statistics/probability strands.

Reader Reliability
The reader reliability rating for the Grade 2 team showed agreement on 15 out of 16 items tested (94%).

Trends in Grade 2 Standards
The heaviest emphasis is placed on continued development of place value and fluency with basic addition and subtraction facts. Measurement focused on telling time and the use of standard units of measure. Geometry primarily focused on 2- and 3-dimensional shapes description. Little emphasis was placed on probability, whereas algebra and data analysis covered primarily work with patterns and collecting, displacing, and interpreting data (mostly from graphs).

Comparison of Second-Grade Standards
The set of standards for which at least 25 percent of the 36 states agreed follows:
Number

    Use multiple representations of base ten number system (31) 86%
    Read and write numbers to X using symbols (26) 72%
    Compare/order numbers to X (25) 69%
    Identify fractions as part of a whole/set (23) 64%
    Represent/model fractions (22) 61%
    Represent numbers; read, write, order, compare (1000) (21) 58%
    Use models (e.g., base ten blocks) (18) 50%
    Identify numbers as odd or even (18) 50%
    Skip count by a given number starting at any number (e.g., Using 100s chart) (17) 47%
    Use expanded notation in words or symbols (16) 44%
    Read and write numbers to X using words (14) 39%
    By composing/decomposing (14) 39%
    Identify and use ordinal number (13) 36%
    Determine the value of a digit based on its position in a number (12) 33%
    Determine the value of a digit based on its position in a number using symbols ($<, >, =$) (11) 31%
    Determine the value of a digit based on its position in a number using words (11) 31%
    Count backwards by 2s, 3s, 5s, and 10s (11) 31%
    Know fractional parts equal to one whole (e.g., 4/4) (10) 28%
    Count by 1s, 2s, 5s, 10s, 100s (or any given number) (9) 25%
    Compare fractions (9) 25%

Number Operations

    Solve problems involving addition and subtraction (29) 81%
    Add and subtract two whole numbers (26) 72%
    Methods/tools for computation (26) 72%
    Fluency with basic facts for addition to 18 (24) 67%
    Fluency with basic facts for subtraction to 18 (24) 67%
    Fluency with basic facts (23) 64%
    Add and subtract two whole numbers with 2 digits (22) 61%
    Methods/tools for computation mental math (20) 56%
    Understand properties commutative property (18) 50%
    Use strategies to estimate sums/quantities (18) 50%
    Understand properties (17) 47%
    Understand properties associative property (17) 47%
    Demonstrate multiplication conceptually (e.g., as repeated addition) (17) 47%
    Methods/tools for computation physical materials/manipulatives (16) 44%
    Understand that addition and subtraction are inverses (15) 42%
    Demonstrate division conceptually (15) 42%
    Add and subtract without regrouping (14) 39%
    Add with regrouping (and subtract) (14) 39%
    Use strategies to estimate sums/quantities to determine reasonableness of answers (e.g., using estimation) (13) 36%
    Use fact families to understand addition and subtraction (9) 25%

Understand properties, identify element (9) 25%
Methods/tools for computation estimation (9) 25%

Measurement

Measure (using standard and nonstandard units) (34) 94%
Tell time to half hour (nearest X minutes) (33) 92%
Measure (using standard and nonstandard units) length (linear) (30) 83%
Estimate (25) 69%
Estimate perimeter or length (linear) in standard and nonstandard units (24) 67%
Select the most appropriate tool or unit to measure an attribute (23) 64%
Make combinations and name total value of coins (21) 58%
Measure (using standard and nonstandard units) customary (21) 58%
Tell time to half hour—analog clocks (17) 47%
Tell time to half hour—digital clocks (17) 47%
Read thermometers (degrees Celsius and/or degrees Fahrenheit) (17) 47%
Measure (using standard and nonstandard units) metric (17) 47%
Measure (using standard and nonstandard units) mass/weight (17) 47%
Estimate weight or mass in kilograms and pounds (16) 44%
Measure (using standard and nonstandard units) capacity/volume (16) 44%
Estimate (using standard and nonstandard units) (15) 42%
Count money through $X (15) 42%
Tell time to nearest 15 minutes (15) 42%
Estimate capacity/volume (14) 39%
Measure (using standard and nonstandard units) to nearest unit (13) 36%
Convert among units in the same system (12) 33%
Tell time to nearest 5 minutes (12) 33%
Linear measurement to nearest inch (11) 31%
Estimate and count the number of units to determine area (10) 28%
Know some simple conversions, hours in day, months in year, etc., regarding time (10) 28%
Use decimals through hundredths with money (10) 28%
Money nearest 1 dollar (10) 28%
Linear measurement nearest centimeter (9) 25%
Tell time to nearest 1 minute (9) 25%

Geometry

Identify/apply symmetry (e.g., lines) (25) 69%
Describe and classify 3-dimensional shapes (24) 67%
Describe attributes of different shapes (e.g., circle, triangle, quadrilaterals) (23) 64%
Combine shapes to form new shape (or subdivide) (21) 58%
Identify and draw congruent shapes (18) 50%
Sort and classify geometric objects (2-dimensional) (16) 44%
Recognize/identify/name 3-dimensional figures (15) 42%
Locate/plot points on a grid or map (12) 33%
Name 2-dimensional objects (11) 31%
Apply transformations—reflections/flips (11) 31%
Identify and apply directionality (north, south, east, west) (11) 31%
Compare shapes using attributes (10) 28%

Apply transformations—rotations/turns (10) 28%
Apply transformations—translations/slides (10) 28%
Identify transformations (10) 28%
Identify shapes from different perspectives (9) 25%
Locate/compare 2-dimensional and 3-dimensional objects in environment (9) 25%

Probability

Predict likelihood of simple events or simple experiments (e.g., certain/impossible, likely/unlikely) (26) 72%
Report probability experiment results (14) 39%
Conduct simple experiments (with 2 outcomes or more) (9) 25%

Data Analysis

Interpret data and draw conclusion (33) 92%
Collect data systematically (29) 81%
Organize and display data (28) 78%
Organize and display data using pictograph (22) 61%
Organize and display data using bar graphs (19) 53%
Organize and display data using tables/charts (17) 47%
Formulate questions from data (16) 44%
Organize and display data using tally chart (13) 36%

Algebra

Extend patterns (31) 86%
Recognize and describe patterns (29) 81%
Create a pattern (20) 56%
Demonstrate equivalency understanding (14) 39%
Describe a rule for a pattern; generalize (13) 36%
Solve an equation with an unknown (10) 28%
Describe qualitative and/or quantitative change (9) 25%

4

Grade 3: Process and Standards

David DeCoste, Chair; *Saint Xavier College, Nova Scotia*
Claudia Ahlstrom, *New Mexico Public Education Department*
Susan Iida, *Sacramento, California*
Anne M. Mikesell, *Ohio Department of Education*

Process
The process used by the Grade 3 team is described in the introduction.

Trends in Grade 3 Standards
The trend seen in the Grade 3 standards is continued computational fluency, beginning computational fluency in multiplication, more work with geometry and algebra, and developing work in data analysis.

Comparison of Third-Grade Standards
The set of standards for which at least 25 percent of the 42 states agreed follows:

Number Sense
Order and compare according to place value (37) 88%
Identify place value with X-digit numbers (34) 81%
Order whole numbers (28) 67%
Understand halves, thirds, fourths, and tenths (28) 67%
Write a whole number up to X (4 or 6) (24) 57%
Model numbers with base 10 blocks (models) (23) 55%
Translate among standard, expanded, and word forms (decompose) (23) 55%
Represent a number up to X in different ways (22) 52%
Model place value with expanded form (19) 45%
Compare two proper fractions with the same denominator (19) 45%
Sort whole numbers as odd or even (19) 45%
Use decimals through tenths and hundredths in context (17) 40%
Skip count by 2s, 5s, 10s (12) 29%

Computation
Compute with 2-, 3-, 4-, or 5-digit numbers in addition and subtraction (33) 79%
Know the relationship between multiplication and repeated addition (29) 69%
Multiply whole numbers with and without regrouping (26) 62%
State multiplication facts through 9s(26) 62%
Illustrate multiplication and division (23) 55%
Demonstrate families of number and division facts through 9s (or 5s) (23) 55%
Explain inverse relationship of multiplication and division (22) 52%
Commutative property (22) 52%
Use mental arithmetic, pencil and paper, or calculator to add and subtract (21) 50%
Know the relationship between division and repeated subtraction (21) 50%

Use estimation strategies (21) 50%
Divide whole numbers using 2-digit dividends and 1-digit divisors (19) 45%
Understand 0 and 1 in addition and multiplication (19) 45%
Know when an approximation is appropriate (15) 36%
Round whole numbers to the nearest X (13) 31%
Associative property (13) 31%
Solve decimal problems (money) (12) 29%
Add or subtract fractions with like denominators, halves, thirds, fourths, eighths, tenths (11) 26%
Reasonable solution (11) 26%
Write number sentences to describe (11) 26%

Algebra

Recognize and extend patterns (39) 93%
Describe the pattern of a number sequence in words (34) 81%
Solve equations with one variable (20) 48%
Solve simple problems with a functional relationship or patterns (20) 48%
Describe, extend, and create patterns using concrete objects (20) 48%
Write mathematical sentences (19) 45%
Identify the rule for a pattern (16) 38%
Represent relations of quantities in the form of expressions, equalities, inequalities (15) 36%
Use properties of whole numbers—commutative (12) 29%
Find missing parts of a pattern (12) 29%
Recognize rule for completing table input/output functions (11) 26%

Measurement

Tell time on a clock to the nearest 15 minutes (28) 67%
Estimate area of figure (26) 62%
Select appropriate units for measuring (25) 60%
Estimate length and weight (23) 55%
Estimate perimeter of figures (21) 50%
Determine elapsed time (21) 50%
Determine perimeter of rectangular shape (19) 45%
Measure temperature to the nearest degree in Fahrenheit and Celsius (19) 45%
Understand the U.S. and metric systems (18) 43%
Estimate and measure volume with unit cubes (14) 33%
Be able to make change with coins (14) 33%
Convert simple measures within a system (12) 29%
Measure length (11) 26%

Geometry/Spatial Sense

Use attributes and properties to work with 2-dimensional figures (35) 83%
Understand how different attributes are used to describe objects (33) 79%
Identify attributes of specified figures (33) 79%
Draw 2-dimensional figures given attributes (32) 76%
Identify a line of symmetry in a 2-dimensional shape (26) 62%
Recognize cubes, cylinders, pyramids, and cones (23) 55%
Compare 2- and 3-dimensional figures by their attributes (23) 55%

Name concrete objects and pictures of 3-dimensional solids (22) 52%
Locate points on a graph (21) 50%
Compare congruent 2-dimensional geometric figures (20) 48%
Determine congruent figures (19) 45%
Identify results of slides, flips, turns of polygons (19) 45%
Build figures with common shapes (18) 43%
Identify solid objects that can make more complex objects (17) 40%
Explain congruence (15) 36%
Determine right and nonright angles (15) 36%
Identify geometric representation for points, lines, perpendicular lines, parallel lines (15) 36%
Identify points in the first quadrant (15) 36%
Follow directions (11) 26%

Data Analysis/Statistics

Make charts and tables—bar (35) 83%
Make charts and tables (32) 76%
Make charts and tables—picture graphs (29) 69%
Pose questions and gather relevant data to answer questions (28) 67%
Apply and explain sampling techniques (tally, observation, polls) (25) 60%
Make inferences based on data (25) 60%
Make charts and tables—line plots or graphs (18) 43%
Interpret graphs for comparative information (16) 38%
Design a survey; collect, and record data (14) 33%
Find mode of a set of data (13) 31%

Probability

Identify events as certain, likely, or unlikely (24) 57%
Determine the likelihood of different outcomes in a simple experiment (21) 50%
Name all outcomes for an experiment (17) 40%

5

Grade 4: Process and Standards

Jeane Joyner, Chair; *Raleigh, North Carolina*
Gail Englert, *School of International Studies at Meadowbrook, Norfolk, Virginia*
Bob Robinson, *Everett, Washington*
Diane L. Schaefer, *Rhode Island Department of Education*

Process
The Grade 4 team used the template to help facilitate the work and basically followed the process described in the introduction.

Reader Reliability
The reader reliability rating for the Grade 4 team showed agreement on 16 out of 16 items tested (100%).

Trends in Grade 4
As will be seen in the list of agreed upon standards, there are more commonalities at Grade 4 than at the earlier grades. Also as seen, more topics are considered in this grade.

Comparison of Fourth-Grade Standards
The set of standards for which at least 25 percent of the 41 states agreed follows:
Number/Number Sense
>Use place value to read and write whole numbers up to X (5–9 digits) (37) 90%
>Model and compare rational numbers (fractions and mixed numbers) (37) 90%
>Order and compare whole numbers (36) 88%
>Identify place value to Xth place to Y thousands (focus on place value ranging from 100,000 to .00001) (35) 85%
>Read and write numbers from Xth place to Y thousands (ranging from 100,000 to 0.00001) (34) 83%
>Describe equivalent fractions (30) 73%
>Compare and order fractions with like denominators (29) 71%
>Compare and order fractions with unlike denominators (28) 68%
>Read, write, and order decimals to Xths (.01 or .001) (28) 68%
>Recognize equivalent forms of whole numbers (27) 66%
>Recognize common fractions as parts of whole (halves, thirds, fourths) (26) 63%
>Represent decimals in different ways (26) 63%
>Determine factors, multiples (19) 46%
>Renaming improper fractions as mixed numbers and vice versa (14) 34%
>Order selected fractions, decimals, and whole numbers on a number line (focus on number line representation) (14) 34%

Determine factors of numbers up to X (where X ranges from small numbers up to 144) (14) 34%

Number Operation/Computation

Use or explain estimation strategies (39) 95%

Multiply X (*n*, 2, or 3) digit numbers by Y (1, 2, or 3) digit numbers (38) 93%

Divide X (*n* - 4) digit number by Y (1 or 2) digit numbers (36) 88%

Solve word problems (34) 83%

Add and subtract with decimals (30) 73%

Know all multiplication and division facts to X times X (where X is up to 12) (28) 68%

Add and subtract fractions with like and unlike denominators (28) 68%

Add and subtract to X digits (from 3 to 6 digits) (25) 61%

Use commutative, associative, and identity properties of addition and multiplication (20) 49%

Determine reasonableness of answers (20) 49%

Use mental computation (19) 46%

Round whole numbers to the nearest Xth place (range from 10s to millions) (18) 44%

Select appropriate operation to solve word problems (15) 37%

Measurement

Use U.S. and metric units to measure (38) 93%

Determine perimeter/area of rectangles (34) 83%

Relate measures within the same system (ID, convert, demonstrate, compare) (31) 76%

Problem-solving situations (see notes page) (29) 70%

Solve problems involving time (elapsed) (27) 66%

Demonstrate conceptual understanding of measurement (selects appropriate tool, unit, etc.) (27) 66%

Use U.S. and metric units to estimate (26) 63%

Compare values and compute money (22) 54%

Use models to determine areas (18) 44%

Differentiate between area and perimeter (16) 39%

Use formulas to determine area and perimeter (16) 39%

Estimate or use protractor to measure angles (14) 34%

Algebra, Patterns, or Functions

Create/extend patterns (31) 76%

Describe/analyze/generalize patterns (finding the rule) (30) 73%

Translate situations into expressions (using letters or symbols as variables) (29) 71%

Solve equations/inequalities (24) 59%

Use or construct function tables (22) 54%

Describe mathematical relationships using constant rate of change (18) 44%

Evaluate algebraic expressions/formulas (18) 44%

Demonstrate equality/inequality (17) 41%

Recognize/use commutativity inverse relationships, order of operations (*see also* – Number/Number Sense) (14) 34%

Geometry

Analyze properties and describe/model/compare 2-dimensional shapes (40) 98%

Analyze properties and describe/model/compare 3-dimensional shapes (37) 90%

Recognize changes resulting from transformations (including tessellations) (36) 88%

Identify/model/draw parallel, perpendicular, intersecting lines/segments (34) 83%

Compare and identify congruent and similar shapes (28) 68%

Identify/model/draw angles (27) 66%

Coordinate graphing (26) 63%

Symmetry (25) 61%

Problem-solving situations (20) 49%

Compose/decompose shapes (12) 29%

Data Analysis/Statistics

Formulate questions; collect, organize, and display data (charts, graphs, tables) (41) 100%

Describe characteristics/analyze data (interpret) (31) 76%

Determine, describe, interpret mean, median, mode, and range (26) 63%

Communicate results; make predictions based on data (22) 54%

Create and solve problems/answer questions based on interpretation of data (looking specifically for "solve problems" or "answer questions") (21) 51%

Classify and describe data in different ways (choose appropriate representation) (15) 37%

Probability

Predict, perform, and record the results of probability experiments (36) 88%

Determine if events are more, less, or equally likely; impossible; or certain (21) 51%

Represent the degree of likelihood using fractions between 0 and 1 (18) 44%

Use counting techniques for combinations and permutations (16) 39%

Determine the theoretical probability for simple experiments through various methods (e.g., tree diagrams) (15) 37%

Problem Solving

Solve real-world problems (11) 27%

Use a variety of strategies to solve a problem (11) 27%

6

Grade 5: Process and Standards

Cindy Bryant, Chair; *Salem, Missouri*
Wesley Bird, *Missouri Department of Education*
Glenn Bruckhart, *Littleton, Colorado*
Robert Kansky, *Cheyenne, Wyoming*
Harvey Keynes, *University of Minnesota*
Barbara Stewart, *Conesus, New York*

Process

The Grade 5 team began with the Number strand, which included number sense and number operation. On the first day, the template standards were read while each team member reviewed a given state's standards to determine if that standard was addressed. If the standard was not listed on the template at any of the 3 levels or a different strand, then the team discussed the standard to determine if at least 4 states had listed it as a standard. If so, the standard was added to the template; if not, it was discarded.

Because this process was very time consuming, it was modified on the second day as follows:

- A strand was selected.
- Each team member was assigned 8 or 9 states.
- Each team member was provided with a copy of the template.
- Each team member reviewed the state documents assigned and looked for matches with the template categories.
- Each state standard was coded as a match with the template or recorded as an item for discussion during the recording and group consensus time.
- Matches were recorded by the team's chair for 4th, 5th, or 6th grade on the template.
- Discussion items (standards listed for a particular state but not listed on the template) were discussed; for each item, a decision was made on whether it matched at a different grade level for that strand, matched a standard in a different strand, or needed to be added to template list for 5th grade. If at least 4 states had listed it as a standard, it was added to the template.

Reader Reliability

The reader reliability rating for the Grade 45 team showed agreement on 14 out of 16 items tested (88%).

Trends in the Grade 5 Standards

Grade 5 common standards can be characterized as a year of fluency with numbers and computation. Measurement and data standards are more in common in Grade 5 than in earlier grades. Another trend seen vividly at this grade level is the number of standards on which there was little agreement. (See these standards in Appendix V.)

Comparison of Fifth-Grade Standards

The set of standards for which at least 25 percent of the 41 states agreed follows:

Number

> Read, write, or represent decimals using symbols, words, or models (28) 68%
>
> Identify or determine equivalent forms of proper fractions (25) 61%
>
> Identify or describe numbers as prime or composite (25) 61%
>
> Find decimal and percent equivalents for common fractions (21) 51%
>
> Compare 2 whole numbers, fractions, and decimals (21) 51%
>
> Read, write, or represent fractions or mixed numbers using symbols, models, and words (20) 49%
>
> Understand the relative magnitude of 1s, 10ths, and 100ths and the relationship of each place value to the place to its right (18) 44%
>
> Compare, order, round, and expand whole numbers through millions and decimals to thousandths (17) 41%
>
> Compare or order fractions with or without using the symbols (<, >, or =) (17) 41%
>
> Compare, order, or describe decimals with or without using the symbols (<, >, or =) (17) 41%
>
> Determine the equivalency between and among fractions, decimals, and percents (15) 37%
>
> Identify a common multiple and the least common multiple (15) 37%
>
> Read, write, and identify common percents (14) 34%
>
> Identify on a number line the relative position of simple positive fractions, positive mixed numbers, and positive decimals (13) 32%
>
> Identify and use rules of divisibility for 2, 3, 4, 5, 6, 9, 10 (13) 32%
>
> Identify numbers less than zero by extending the number line (11) 27%
>
> Understand percentages as parts out of 100, use percent notation, and express a part of a whole as a percentage (11) 27%

Number Operation

> Use estimation to verify the reasonableness of a calculation (28) 68%
>
> Add and subtract decimals (26) 63%
>
> Add and subtract fractions (including mixed numbers) with different denominators (25) 61%
>
> Solve arithmetic problems using estimation (22) 54%
>
> Divide 3-digit numbers by a single digit (21) 51%
>
> Add and subtract fractions with like denominators (20) 49%
>
> Multiply 2-digit numbers by 2-digit numbers (18) 44%
>
> Round to estimate quantities (16) 39%
>
> Demonstrate computational fluency with addition, subtraction, multiplication, and division of whole numbers (15) 37%
>
> Identify such properties as commutativity, associativity, and distributivity and use them to compute with whole numbers (15) 37%
>
> Add, subtract, multiply, and divide decimals (13) 32%
>
> Determine from real-world problems whether an estimated or exact answer is acceptable (12) 29%
>
> Use models to show an understanding of multiplication and division of fractions (11) 27%

Measurement

Convert measurement units to equivalent units within a given system (U.S. customary and metric) (23) 56%

Determine perimeter (22) 54%

Select and use appropriate tools and units (18) 44%

Determine area (18) 44%

Determine start, elapsed, and end time (15) 37%

Determine volumes (15) 37%

Estimate and determine weight (13) 32%

Estimate volumes (12) 29%

Solve problems using perimeter, area, and volume (12) 29%

Measure in customary and metric units (11) 27%

Measure angles (11) 27%

Estimate area (11) 27%

Estimate and determine length (11) 27%

Geometry

Identify the properties of 2- and 3-dimensional geometric figures using appropriate terminology and vocabulary (29) 71%

Analyze the properties of plane geometric figures (24) 59%

Predict the results of a flip (reflection), turn (rotation), or slide (translation) (18) 44%

Compare or classify triangles by sides or angle measures (17) 41%

Identify shapes that have reflectional and rotational symmetry (16) 39%

Identify congruent figures and demonstrate your decisions by referring to sides and angles (14) 34%

Probability

Predict and explain the probability of all possible outcomes in an experiment using ratios or fractions (22) 54%

Understand that probability has value between 0 and 1 inclusive: unlikely events have probability 0; certain events have probability 1; and likely events have a higher probability than less likely ones (12) 29%

Data Analysis

Find the mean, median, mode, and range of a set of data and describe what each does and does not tell about the data set (34) 83%

Read and interpret tables, charts, and graphs (including stem-and-leaf, histogram, bar graph, pie graph, box and whiskers, line graph, scatter plots) (25) 61%

Organize and construct tables, charts, and graphs (22) 54%

Collect data using measurements, surveys, or experiments and represent the data with tables and graphs with labeling (21) 51%

Explain which types of displays are appropriate for various sets of data (20) 49%

Formulate reasonable predictions from a given set of data (12) 29%

Algebra

Identify, describe, extend, and create numeric patterns from shapes, tables, and graphs (29) 71%

Use a variable to represent an unknown number (27) 66%

Analyze and generalize number patterns and state a rule for relationships (20) 49%

Plot points on a 1-quadrant grid (18) 44%

Describe a rule used in a simple grade-level appropriate function (18) 44%

Evaluate algebraic expressions with 1 unknown, 1 operation, and whole numbers (14) 34%

Find the value of the unknown in an equation using 1 operation (14) 34%

Identify, describe, extend, and create functions from shapes, tables, and graphs (13) 32%

Write simple algebraic expressions in one or two variables (13) 32%

Make and use coordinate systems to specify locations/objects and to describe paths (11) 27%

7

Grade 6: Process and Standards

Barbara Reys, Chair; *University of Missouri—Columbia*
Carolyn Baldree, *Georgia Department of Education*
Donna Taylor, *North Carolina Department of Public Instruction*
Stephen Wilson, *Johns Hopkins University*

Process

To begin, each member of the Grade 6 team took a state document, focusing on one strand. As a group, the team discussed each item (i.e., learning expectation) on the template for that strand to ensure a common understanding among the team members. Then the team began searching within state documents for learning expectations noted on the template. As expectations were located, they were read aloud so that a group decision could be made as to whether the expectation matched a template item. This group coding was done for 12 states until the team was in general agreement on the task for the strand.

After the group review, team members began individually summarizing state documents, asking for assistance as needed to clarify particular expectations found in the state documents. When all state documents were coded in one strand, another strand was chosen to review.

On review of the limited number of "process" standards for states, the team determined that few states had process standards unique to Grade 6. As a result, the process standards were not coded for Grade 6.

Reader Reliability
The reader reliability rating for the Grade 6 team showed agreement on 15 out of 16 items tested (94%).

Trends in the Grade 6 Standards
The Grade 6 team suggested the following trends from their review of the 41 state documents. The trends are summarized by strand. The number of states specifying a given standard is listed in parentheses.

Number and Operation
The largest set of learning expectations for Grade 6 is in this strand. Common learning expectations include the following:
- Compute with fractions and decimals (39)
- Compare and order fractions and decimals (34)
- Locate numbers on a number line (26)
- Identify least common multiple and greatest common factor (25)
- Express a number in its prime factorization (24)
- Determine the equivalency among fractions, decimals, and percents (23)
- Use order of operations (22)

Algebra

Learning expectations represent introductory experiences with simple equations. Common learning expectations include the following:
- Solve linear equations in 1 unknown (31)
- Create function tables and graphs (22)
- Continue patterns (25)

Geometry

Common learning expectations include the following:
- Classify and compare quadrilaterals based on attributes (28)
- Classify and compare triangles based on attributes (24)
- Identify and use congruent, similar, and symmetrical geometric figures (23)

Measurement

Common learning expectations include the following:
- Convert units within a system (30)
- Select appropriate units and tools of measure (29)
- Measure perimeter and area (27)
- Develop and use formulas for perimeter and area (22)
- Measure area of triangles and quadrilaterals (21)

Data Analysis

Common learning expectations include the following:
- Find and use the mean, median, and range of a set of data (33)
- Interpret information from bar graphs, line graphs, and circle graphs (32)
- Construct different kinds of graphs (e.g., line, double bar, circle) (28)

Probability

Common learning expectations include the following:
- Find the probability of a single event (24)

Comparison of Sixth-Grade Standards

The set of standards for which at least 25 percent of the 41 states agreed follows:

Number

Compare and order integers, fractions, decimals, and mixed numbers (35) 85%

Locate numbers (whole, fractions, integers, or decimals) on a number line (26) 63%

Use greatest common factor (divisor) (26) 63%

Express a number in its prime factorization (25) 61%

Use least common multiple (25) 61%

Determine equivalency among fractions, decimals, mixed numbers, and percents (22) 54%

Use exponential powers (18) 44%

Use and understand decimals (18) 44%

Identify primes and composite numbers (17) 41%

Understand and use integers (16) 39%

Use different forms to symbolize ratios or rates (15) 37%

Convert among fractions and decimals (14) 34%
Use percent to represent a part of a whole (14) 34%
Use integers to describe real-world phenomena (13) 32%
Understand fractions as ratios (13) 32%
Understand and apply the concept of negative numbers (12) 29%
Simplify fractions to lowest terms (12) 29%
Convert among fractions and percents (11) 27%
Convert among decimals and percents (11) 27%

Number Operations

Compute with fractions (39) 95%
Compute with decimals (34) 83%
Estimate the reasonableness of results (25) 61%
Use order of operations (22) 54%
Estimate results of computations (22) 54%
Estimate with fractions and decimals (18) 44%
Meaning of operations, modeling of operations (18) 44%
Describe and illustrate commutative, associative, inverse, and identity properties for addition and multiplication (16) 39%
Find percent of number (16) 39%
Round numbers using a variety of techniques (15) 37%
Understand relations among basic operations (13) 32%
Compute with positive and negative numbers (12) 29%

Measurement

Convert units of length, weight, capacity within a system (30) 73%
Select appropriate unit of measure or tool (29) 71%
Estimate or measure perimeter of figures (27) 66%
Develop and use formulas for perimeter and area (22) 54%
Estimate or measure area of triangles or quadrilaterals (20) 49%
Find the circumference of a circle (19) 46%
Find angle measure (17) 41%
Create a new figure by increasing or decreasing original measures (scale drawing) (17) 41%
Measure to the nearest X unit (16) 39%
Find the volume of selected 3-dimensional figures (15) 37%
Determine distance between two points on a scale drawing (12) 29%

Geometry

Classify or compare quadrilaterals based on attributes (28) 68%
Classify triangles by angles (24) 59%
Identify and use congruent, similar, or symmetrical geometric figures (23) 56%
Classify angles by measure (20) 49%
Find or draw the results of transformations on a figure (20) 49%
Identify spheres, cones, cylinders, prisms, and pyramids (18) 44%
Identify or draw 2-dimensional views of 3-dimensional figures (15) 37%
Identify rotational symmetries (15) 37%
Identify and use parts of a circle (13) 32%
Identify line symmetries (13) 32%

Probability
       Find the probability of a simple event (24) 59%
       Express probabilities as ratios, percents, and decimals (18) 44%
       Name all possible outcomes from an experiment (16) 39%
       Determine the theoretical probability of a given event (13) 32%
       Make predictions using probability (13) 32%

Data Analysis
       Find and use mean, median, mode, range (33) 80%
       Interpret information from bar graphs, line graphs, and circle graphs (32) 78%
       Construct histogram, line graph, scatter plot, stem-and-leaf plot, double bar graphs, tally charts, frequency tables, circle graphs, line graphs, box-and-whisker plots (28) 68%
       Choose appropriate representations (18) 44%
       Design an investigation; collect, organize, and display data (16) 39%
       Formulate questions from contextual data (12) 29%

Algebra
       Solve an equation for an unknown; linear equation, one unknown (30) 73%
       Continue a pattern (25) 61%
       Create functions tables and graphs (22) 54%
       Use variables in contexts (20) 49%
       Plot coordinates (20) 49%
       Determine a verbal rule for a function given input and output (19) 46%
       Identify coordinates in Cartesian plane (17) 41%
       Express rules with and without variables (15) 37%
       Translate between words and symbols (14) 34%
       Explain how change in one variable relates to another variable (14) 34%
       Simplify expressions using order of operations (11) 27%
       Evaluate an expression by substitution (11) 27%

8
Grade 7: Process and Standards

Jennie Bennett, Chair; *Houston, Texas*
Judith Keeley, *Rhode Island Department of Education*
Andy Magid, *University of Oklahoma*
Sarah F. Mason, *Alabama Department of Education*
Paula Moeller, *Texas Education Agency*
Carolyn Sessions, *Louisiana Department of Education*

Process

The Grade 7 team discussed the strand headings and expectations in the template to ensure a common understanding among the members of the Grade 7 team. As a group, the team members took a state document and focused on one strand. The expectation was read aloud from the template. Team members examined the state document to determine if the learning expectation in that strand matched the template item. Group discussions and decisions were made on the basis of whether the expectation matched the template item.

Following the discussion and decisions about a strand item, the item was coded on the template. Once team members completed reviewing all state documents in a strand and coding the item, another strand was chosen for review.

The team had an extensive discussion regarding the process standards for states. The team determined that only a small number of states had a separate section of expectations called "process standards" for Grade 7. The team coded a process standard on the template if it was determined that the standard was embedded with other strands. The team additionally identified process expectations that were not indicated on the template for Grade 7.

Reader Reliability

The reader reliability rating for the Grade 7 team showed agreement on 14 out of 16 items tested (88%).

Trends for Grade 7 Standards

With the strand Number and Operations, the Grade 7 team found that states tend to emphasize fractions, decimals, and percents. In Measurement, conversions in the same system, finding perimeter, and finding area were prominent. In Geometry, properties of figures were evident as were graphing on coordinate plane and work with two- and three-dimensional figures. In Probability, predictions of results of experiments dominated. In Data Analysis, the use of mean, median, mode, and range were primary, with mention of quartiles and interquartile range. Graphical representations of collected data were also evident. In the Algebra strand, work with patterns, including extending patterns, and developing tables, solving one- and two-step equations, and inequalities with some work on simplifying expressions were seen, as well as an introduction to linear patterns.

The Grade 7 team looked at process standards, such as problem solving, connections, reasoning, and communications. Some states, such as Texas, Utah, Alaska, Idaho, Washington, Indiana, Georgia, Nevada, Arizona, Minnesota, Oregon, California, Colorado, and Maryland, as well as the Department of Defense Education Agency have separate strands with the process standards. States with embedded process standards include Alabama, Louisiana, Arizona, Florida, North Carolina, Ohio, Mississippi, Missouri, Virginia, Kansas, South Dakota, North Dakota, Michigan, New Hampshire, West Virginia, Kentucky, Wyoming, Tennessee, and Montana, as well as the District of Columbia. In all states, the team identified problem solving in real-world settings; reasoning to obtain, justify, and defend solutions; connections inside and outside mathematics; and written and oral communication to express mathematical ideas and in a variety of settings. Additionally, the team found the use of technology both embedded and separately; however, there was not enough information to categorize the standards in this arena.

Comparison of Seventh-Grade Standards
The set of standards for which at least 25 percent of the 42 states agreed follows:
Number
Identify and convert between equivalent forms of rational numbers (19) 45%

Write, compare, and solve problems using scientific notation (16) 38%

Find the prime factorization of whole numbers (16) 38%

Fractions, decimals, irrational numbers in nondecimal form (15) 36%

Place numbers in position on a number line (15) 36%

Find the greatest common factor (15) 36%

Demonstrate an understanding of rational numbers: fractions, decimals, percents, integers (14) 33%

Order and compare numbers (14) 33%

Locate integers on a number line (13) 31%

Identify and use primes and composites (12) 29%

Find the least common multiple (11) 26%

Demonstrate divisibility rules for X (11) 26%

Number Operations
Use order of operations (24) 57%

Rational numbers: integers, fractions, and terminating decimals (20) 48%

Use properties of operations—commutative (20) 48%

Use properties of operations—associative (20) 48%

Use percents to solve problems (20) 48%
proportion (20) 48%

Use properties of operations (18) 43%

Use properties of operations—identity (18) 43%

Use properties of operations—inverse (17) 40%

Use properties of operations—distributive property of multiplication over addition (17) 40%

Convert among standard forms and scientific notation (16) 38%

Understand and apply the concept of square roots (15) 36%

Select and justify the appropriate computation strategy (15) 36%

Determine reasonableness of results (15) 36%

Add, subtract, multiply, and divide with fluency (14) 33%

Compute absolute value (13) 31%

Use inverse properties of addition and multiplication (12) 29%

Evaluate powers (12) 29%

Find square roots (11) 26%

Measurement

Find the area of polygons and/or circles (24) 57%

Choose appropriate units of measure (21) 50%

Measure using tools (18) 43%

Find the circumference of circles (18) 43%

Use formulas to find perimeter, area, volume (18) 43%

Determine surface area of 3-dimensional figures (17) 40%

Convert units of length, weight, or capacity from metric to customary and vice versa (16) 38%

Find the perimeter of polygons (12) 29%

Know how perimeter, area, and volume are affected by change of scale (12) 29%

Estimate measures of length, area, or volume (11) 26%

Geometry

Graph points on a coordinate plane (25) 60%

Identify, describe, compare, and sort geometric figures (22) 52%

Determine transformations to move polygons on plane (22) 52%

Investigate properties and relationships among congruent or similar figures (18) 43%

Identify basic attributes/properties of geometric figures (16) 38%

Construct geometric figures with different tools (14) 33%

Describe results of transformations (12) 29%

Know angle relationships with different types of lines (11) 26%

Probability

Predict results of experiments (18) 43%

Distinguish between experimental and theoretical probabilities (14) 33%

Data Analysis

Mean (30) 71%

Median (30) 71%

Mode (28) 67%

Range (26) 62%

Collect, organize, display data in circle graphs (24) 57%

Collect, organize, display data (23) 55%

Collect, organize, display data in stem-and-leaf plots (20) 48%

Collect, organize, display data in scatter plots (17) 40%

Box-and-whisker plots and outliers (16) 38%

Collect, organize, display data in histograms (15) 36%

Draw conclusions (15) 36%

Formulate questions about data (14) 33%

Collect, organize, display data in bar graphs (14) 33%

Collect, organize, display data in line graphs (14) 33%

Interpret trends from displayed data (12) 29%

Collect, organize, display data in frequency tables (11) 26%

Tables (11) 26%

Algebra

Solve equations: 1 step (27) 64%

Evaluate expressions (24) 57%

Express a pattern shown in a table; graph as an equation or expression (19) 45%

Solve inequalities (18) 43%
Determine an expression that represents a situation (16) 38%
Extend patterns (15) 36%
Identify linear patterns (15) 36%
Describe a rule for a pattern (11) 26%
Identify and extend an arithmetic sequence (11) 26%
Identify and extend a geometric sequence (11) 26%

Problem Solving

Problem solving and explanations in real-world settings (42) 100%

Reasoning

Use mathematical reasoning to obtain, justify, defend solutions (41) 98%

Connections

Makes connections within and outside of mathematics (42) 100%

Communications

Express mathematical ideas written, orally using a variety of methods (e.g., modeling) (42) 100%

9

Grade 8: Process and Standards

Laurie Boswell, Chair; *Monroe, New Hampshire*
Jerry Dancis, *University of Maryland*
Michael Kestner, *U.S. Department of Education*
Frank Marburger, *Pennsylvania Department of Education*
Lois Williams, *Virginia Department of Education*

Process

The Grade 8 team began with the Number strand, a very long strand at this grade level. On the first day, the template standards were read by cluster while each team member reviewed a given 2 to 3 state's standards to determine if that standard was addressed. Coding was performed as directed by conference leaders. This process was repeated until all states had been coded for that cluster of standards. If the standard was not listed on the template, the team discussed the standard to determine if at least 4 states had listed it as a standard. If so, the standard was added to the template; if not, it was discarded.

This process was very time consuming and was modified on the second day as follows:

- A strand was selected; the team discussed the language of each standard within the strand; some standards were combined using language agreed to by all team members.
- Each team member was assigned 8 to 9 states.
- Each team member had a copy of the template.
- Each team member reviewed the assigned state documents and looked for matches with the template standards.
- Each state standard was coded as a match with the template or recorded as an item for discussion during the recording and group consensus time.

Discussion items (standards listed for a particular state but not listed on the template) were discussed and a decision was made on whether they matched at a different grade level for that strand, matched a different strand, or needed to be added to template list for eighth grade. If at least 4 states had listed it as a standard, it was added to the template.

Reader Reliability

The reader reliability rating for the Grade 8 team showed agreement on 14 out of 16 items tested (88%).

Trends for Grade 8 Standards

The majority of states organized their standards by strands as does NCTM in *Principles and Standards for School Mathematics* (2000). Many states have a more complete list of content items in number and numeration than in other strands. Virtually all the states had content on rational numbers. In the collection of standards, classical Algebra I content is apparent even in states where there may be no Algebra I course.

The Grade 8 team found that the style of state standards made it very hard to judge completeness or incompleteness of standards and mathematics involved. Some states repeated content in each of the Grade 7, Grade 8, and Grade 9 standards. Other states appeared to assume mastery and expect maintenance and did not have all standards written. A suggestion from this team to standards writers is to identify new content and indicate when mastery is expected. The team further suggested that standards be presented graphically in a concept map to show concept development.

The Grade 8 team followed the lead of the Grade 7 team on observations about process standards. In the area of technology, the team found that most states were not clear about whether use was expected.

Comparison of Eighth-Grade Standards

The set of standards for which at least 25 percent of the 39 states agreed follows:

Number

   Understand and use ratio and proportion (29) 74%
   Write numbers using scientific notation (28) 72%
   Solve problems using estimation (26) 67%
   Understand and use percents (23) 59%
   Calculate the missing value in a percentage problem (23) 59%
   Order real numbers (22) 56%
   Simplify numerical expressions using the order of operations (21) 54%
   Apply appropriate properties to assist in computation (19) 49%
   Verify the reasonableness of a solution (19) 49%
   Locate numbers on a number line (16) 41%
   Use alternative representations for rational numbers (15) 38%
   Determine whether a number is rational or irrational (15) 38%
   Understand and use inverse operations (15) 38%
   Apply properties of real numbers (commutative, associative, distributive, identity,
       equality, inverse, closure) (15) 38%
   Demonstrate computational fluency with operations on rational numbers (14) 36%
   Understand and use the distributive property (14) 36%
   Understand and use exponential notation (13) 33%
   Explain when an approximation is appropriate (13) 33%
   Apply greatest common factor, least common multiple, prime and composite numbers in
       finding results (10) 26%
   Write prime factorization of numbers (10) 26%
   Use primes, factors, multiples, divisibility rules (10) 26%
   Perform all operations on real numbers (10) 26%

Measurement

   Determine the surface area and volume of solid figures (35) 90%
   Find the area and perimeter of regular and irregular figures (23) 59%
   Convert within a measuring system (19) 49%
   Estimate measures (17) 44%
   Determine appropriate units of measure for surface area and volume (13) 33%
   Use measurement techniques to find indirect measures (13) 33%
   Determine measures of angles and angle pairs (11) 28%

Develop formulas for surface areas and volumes of prisms, cylinders, and pyramids (11) 28%

Approximate distance or height using similar figures or triangles to solve problems (10) 26%

Geometry

Solve problems using the Pythagorean theorem (35) 90%

Identify corresponding angles of similar polygons as congruent and sides as proportional, corresponding parts–figures, and solve problems (22) 56%

Compare quadrilaterals, triangles, and solids using properties and characteristics (20) 51%

Use dilations on the coordinate plane to determine measures of similar figures (19) 49%

Use the results of transformations to find congruent figures (16) 41%

Use 2-dimensional nets to construct 3-dimensional figures (15) 38%

Construct and use scale drawings (13) 33%

Model a transformation on a coordinate grid (12) 31%

Identify parts of triangles, for example, angle bisectors (11) 28%

Probability

Counting techniques (20) 51%

Compare theoretical and experimental probability (19) 49%

Compute the probability of independent and dependent events (14) 36%

Determine the probability of an event by simulation (13) 33%

Data Analysis

Interpret data from populations, using given and collected data (27) 69%

Represent data with the most appropriate graph (20) 51%

Determine the measure of center that is most appropriate (18) 46%

Formulate reasonable predictions based on a given set of data (18) 46%

Make predictions by estimating the line of best fit from a scatter plot (15) 38%

Represent data with the most appropriate graph—scatter plot (14) 36%

Recognize when a sample is biased (14) 36%

Represent data with the most appropriate graph—box-and-whisker plot (12) 31%

Represent data with the most appropriate graph—circle graph (10) 26%

Evaluate the effects of missing or incorrect data on results of an investigation (10) 26%

Know when probability and statistics are misused (10) 26%

Sampling techniques (10) 26%

Algebra

Identify functions from information in tables, sets of order pairs, equations, graphs, and mappings (33) 85%

Solve problems using linear functions (27) 69%

Solve 2-step linear equations (25) 64%

Graph linear relations by plotting points or by using slope-intercept form (19) 49%

Describe how a change in one variable affects a related variable (17) 44%

Determine slopes and y-intercepts of lines (17) 44%

Classify relations as linear or nonlinear (15) 38%

Translate a written phrase into an algebraic expression (15) 38%

Solve linear inequalities (14) 36%

Describe and extend patterns to the nth term (12) 31%

Use order of operations to simplify algebraic expressions (12) 31%
Evaluate algebraic expressions by substituting rational values for variables (12) 31%
Identify an equation or inequality that represents a contextual situation (12) 31%
Solve systems of equations (12) 31%
Graph an inequality on a number line (10) 26%
Find equivalent equations (10) 26%

Problem Solving

Problem solving (30) 77%
Communication (22) 56%
Reasoning (20) 51%
Connections (18) 46%

10

Grade 9: Process and Standards—Algebra

Rick Jennings, Chair; *Washington State Office of the Department of Public Instruction*
Ann Bartosh, *Kentucky Department of Education*
Daniel Dolan, *Cromwell, Connecticut*
Linda Hackett, *Department of Education Agency*
Roger Howe, *Yale University*
Anthony Scott, *Chicago, Illinois*

Process

The Grade 9 team identified each state that had standards listed as Grade 9 Standards, Algebra I Standards, or Integrated Mathematics I Standards. The identified state standards were then used for analysis. Because so few states had standards at Grade 9 and integrated mathematics I, those standards are in Appendix V.

Standards for each state were read and matched to the template if present. If a particular standard was not on the template, the team added the standard on a Post-it® note listing the states that included the standard. This identified standards that were either close to, or more expansive than, a template standard. The notes were compiled and incorporated into the summary report.

Reader Reliability

The reader reliability rating for the Grade 9 team showed agreement on 15 out of 16 items tested (94%).

Trends in Grade 9 Standards

The team found the following trends:

- Integrated Mathematics I: This course is inconsistent across states. It appeared that the use of strands in standards worked against the use of integration. In fact, the Algebra I course seemed more integrated than not and had more integrated-type topics than did the Integrated Math I course.

- Algebra I seemed to have less on functions listed as standards than were needed. The dominant standard regarding functions in Algebra I was to determine characteristics of functions.

Comparison of Algebra I Course Standards

In the past, Algebra I has typically been considered a Grade 9 course. The placement of the course is changing in many states. However, even with the change in grade level where it is taught, the course content has changed little. As a result, the course standards for Algebra I are placed under Grade 9 regardless of the grade level at which the course is offered.

Comparison of Ninth-Grade Algebra I Course Standards

The set of standards for which at least 25 percent of the 16 states agreed follows:

Number and Operations

Apply laws of exponents (6) 38%

Simplify expressions (5) 31%

Simplify square roots using factors (5) 31%

Measurement

Solve problems algebraically (5) 31%

Solve problems algebraically that involve area of a polygon and a circle (5) 31%

Solve problems algebraically that involve volume of cylinders, prisms (5) 31%

Solve problems algebraically that involve perimeter of a polygon, circumference of a circle (4) 25%

Algebra

Interpret a graph representing a given situation (16) 100%

Solve linear inequalities (15) 94%

Solve one-variable equations (14) 88%

Study slope as a rate of change (12) 75%

Determine characteristics of a relation (11) 69%

Determine characteristics of a relation including domain (11) 69%

Determine characteristics of a relation including range (11) 69%

Perform arithmetic operations on polynomials (10) 63%

Determine equation of line (10) 63%

Model real-world problems by developing and solving equations and inequalities (10) 63%

Solve a quadratic equation by factoring or completing the square (10) 63%

Graph quadratic functions and know that their roots are the x-intercepts (10) 63%

Determine characteristics of a relation including if it is a function (9) 56%

Determine equation of line given a point and the slope (9) 56%

Find the slope of a line from its equation (8) 50%

Determine equation of line given 2 points (8) 50%

Determine equation of line given graphs (8) 50%

Graph two-variable linear equations and inequalities on the Cartesian plane (8) 50%

Use the quadratic formula to find the roots of a second-degree polynomial and to solve equations (8) 50%

Recognize and represent number patterns algebraically (7) 44%

Describe changes in graphs that correspond to changes in parameters of $y = mx + b$ (7) 44%

Solve systems of linear equations and inequalities in two variables, graphically or algebraically (7) 44%

Apply the addition, multiplication, and equality axioms of real numbers to simplify expressions (6) 38%

Determine equation of line given tables of values (6) 38%

Calculate length, midpoint, and slope of a line segment (6) 38%

Solve a system of linear equations by graphing, substitution, or elimination (6) 38%

Solve multistep equations and inequalities, including linear, radical, absolute value, and literal equations (6) 38%

Translate among different representations of functions and relations (6) 38%

Translate among different representations of functions and relations: Graphs (6) 38%

Translate among different representations of functions and relations: Tabular (6) 38%

Translate words into expressions and equations and vice versa (5) 31%

Factor polynomials (5) 31%

Analyze linear functions from their equations, slopes, and intercepts (5) 31%

Find the slope of a line by applying the slope formula (5) 31%

Know the quadratic formula and are familiar with its proof by completing the square (5) 31%

Translate among different representations of functions and relations: Equations (5) 31%

Represent situations with the following: Linear function (4) 25%

Represent relations graphically (4) 25%

Evaluate polynomials (4) 25%

Determine equation of line given ordered pairs (4) 25%

Use slope to differentiate among lines that are parallel, perpendicular, vertical, and horizontal (4) 25%

Solve open sentences (4) 25%

Translate among different representations of functions and relations: Point sets (4) 25%

Data Analysis

Collect and organize data (7) 44%

Make inferences and predictions (7) 44%

Use a scatter plot and its line of best fit or a specific line graph to determine the relationship existing between 2 sets of data (6) 38%

Identifies measure of central tendency including standard deviation (6) 38%

Use technology to find the line or curve of best fit (4) 25%

Problem Solving

Decide whether a solution is reasonable (5) 31%

Solve problems using direct, inverse, and joint variation (5) 31%

Use a variety of strategies (4) 25%

Probability

Compare theoretical and experimental probabilities (4) 25%

11

Grade 10: Process and Standards—Geometry

Richard Seitz, Chair; *Helena, Montana*
Deborah Bliss, *Virginia Department of Education*
Margaret Bondorew, *Foxboro, Massachusetts*
Scott Eddins, *Tennessee Department of Education*
Jerry Evans, *Utah Department of Education*
William McCallum, *University of Arizona*

Process

The Grade 10 team had a designated team member read a standard. Once read, other team members examined assigned parts of the template for a match to the standard that had been read. The process described in the introduction was used to reach consensus.

Reader Reliability

The reader reliability rating for the Grade 10 team showed agreement on 15 out of sixteen items tested (94%).

Trends in Grade 10 Standards

There seems to be little or no consistency in what constitutes the body of knowledge for Grade 10 Integrated Mathematics II; these standards are seen in Appendix V. This is not the case for geometry. The body of knowledge that constitutes high school geometry seems to be fairly consistent.

Inclusion of topics from probability, statistics, and discrete mathematics in high school algebra and geometry courses adds disparity to the content in courses across states. Content topics were fairly consistent across state standards and other documents, but the use of verbs to incorporate process standards in content standards is problematic.

Comparison of Tenth-Grade Geometry Standards

The set of standards for which at least 25 percent of the 14 states agreed follows:

Algebra

Apply distance, midpoint, and slope formulas to solve problems and to confirm properties of polygons (6) 43%

Determine the equation of a line parallel or perpendicular to a second line through a given point (5) 36%

Find the equation of a circle in a coordinate plane (5) 36%

Find the lengths and midpoints of segments in 1- and 2-dimension using coordinates and find slopes (4) 29%

Properties of Figures

Classify and use (apply) types of angles formed by 2 lines and a transversal (10) 71%

Verify the relationships among different classes of polygons using their properties (6) 43%

Identify and describe convex, concave, and regular polygons (5) 36%

Identify and describe types of triangles (4) 29%

Constructions

Perform basic constructions with straightedge and compass (10) 71%

Using Geometry

Determine the measure of interior and exterior angles associated with polygons (8) 57%

Apply the Pythagorean theorem to solve application problems (8) 57%

Apply ratios and proportions to find missing parts of similar polygons (7) 50%

Find the sums of the measures of the interior and exterior angles of a polygon (6) 43%

Determine the missing lengths of sides or measures of angles in similar polygons (5) 36%

Solve real-life and mathematical problems using properties and theorems (4) 29%

Solve real-life and mathematical problems using properties and theorems related to quadrilaterals (4) 29%

Trigonometry

Use trigonometric functions to find unknowns (11) 79%

Know the definitions of basic trigonometric functions (10) 71%

Use the ratios of the sides of special right triangles to find lengths of missing sides (8) 57%

Find the missing measures of sides and angles in right triangles using trigonometry and solve problems (5) 36%

Measurement

Calculate surface areas and volumes of solid figures (13) 93%

Calculate surface areas and volumes of solid figures: Cones and cylinders (13) 93%

Calculate surface areas and volumes of solid figures: Pyramids (13) 93%

Calculate surface areas and volumes of solid figures: Spheres (13) 93%

Calculate surface areas and volumes of solid figures: Prisms (12) 86%

Calculate the measures of arcs and sectors of circle (9) 64%

Find and use area of polygons and circles (8) 57%

Find and use perimeter or circumference of geometric figures (7) 50%

Find and use the surface areas of solids (7) 50%

Find and use the volumes of solids (6) 43%

Transformations

Apply transformations to polygons to determine congruence, similarity, symmetry, and tessellations (5) 36%

Use length and area models to determine probability and volume (5) 36%

Know the effect of rigid motions and dilations on figures (4) 29%

Reasoning

Use inductive reasoning to make conjectures and deductive reasoning to justify conclusions (11) 79%

Use of/justify theorems related to congruence (11) 79%

Use of/justify theorems related to properties of parallel and perpendicular lines (10) 71%

Use of/justify theorems related to relationships among chords, secants, tangents, inscribed angles, and both inscribed and circumscribed polygons of circles (10) 71%

Use of/justify theorems (9) 64%

Use of/justify theorems related to pairs of angles (8) 57%

Use of/justify theorems related to similarity (8) 57%

Use of/justify theorems related to properties of quadrilaterals (7) 50%

Use of/justify theorems related to properties of circles (7) 50%

Write geometric proofs (7) 50%

Deduce relationships between two triangles, including proving congruence or similarity (6) 43%

Prove theorems using coordinate geometry (6) 43%

Prove and use the triangle inequality theorems: triangle inequality, inequality in one triangle (6) 43%

Identify the converse, inverse, and contrapositive of a conditional statement (6) 43%

Construct and judge the validity of a logical argument (5) 36%

Write proofs by contradiction (5) 36%

Identify and give examples of undefined terms, axioms, theorems, and inductive and deductive reasoning (4) 29%

Give counterexamples to disprove a statement (4) 29%

12

Grade 11: Process and Standards—Algebra II, Precalculus

M. Kathleen Heid, Chair; *Penn State University*
David Brancamp, *Nevada Department of Education*
Jerry Dwyer, *Texas Tech University*
David Hoff, *Bottineau, North Dakota*
James Rubillo, *National Council of Teachers of Mathematics*

Process

The Grade 11 team noted that not all state standards could be examined in the same way. Standards from states were separated into two major categories: (1) those states with standards organized by grade level or grade band, and (2) those states with standards organized by high school courses. The Grade 11 team began by looking at the "grade-level" standards at each strand (i.e., Number and Operations, Algebra), and then looked at the states with standards for "named" courses, such as Algebra II and precalculus. The entire team looked at the template and discussed areas in which ideas could be combined to form a larger or expanded idea, and then revised the template accordingly.

If a state's standard contained an idea from the template, the team coded the standard using the process outlined in the introduction.

Reader Reliability

The reader reliability rating for the Grade 11 team showed agreement on 15 out of 16 items tested (94%).

Trends in Algebra II Standards

The Grade 11 team concluded the following about the Algebra II course:
- A moderate emphasis is placed on sequences and series, quadratic inequalities, rational expressions, solution of quadratics with complex numbers, and the fundamental counting principle with combinations and permutations.
- A heavy emphasis is placed on the algebra of functions, including operations on functions, composition, and inverses; linear and quadratic functions (with some work on families of functions); and linear equations and inequalities.

The Grade 11 team concluded the following about the precalculus course:
- Major similarities in this course's standards exist in the analysis of functions beyond linear and quadratic types, sequences and series, modeling using a variety of functional techniques, solving higher order equations, and conic sections and vectors. Trigonometry was a common topic; however, apart from graphing, major differences were found on topics in the area of trigonometry.
- Major differences exist in the level of data analysis done in this course, and major differences were also found in the rigor of proof.

Almost none of the process standards are found in Grade 11; technology is noted weakly.

Comparisons of Eleventh-Grade Algebra II Course Standards
The following comparisons involve standards for which at least 25 percent of the 14 states agreed:
Number and Operations
> Define, represent, and use complex numbers (12) 86%
> Perform operations with complex numbers (10) 71%
> Simplify radicals and expressions involving fractional exponents and convert between the two forms (7) 50%
> Interpret symbolic notation (5) 36%
> Adds, subtracts scalar multiples, and multiplies matrices (5) 36%
> Factor polynomials (4) 29%

Algebra
> Solve systems of linear inequalities and equations (12) 86%
> Solve quadratic equations over the set of complex numbers (11) 79%
> Define a function using domain (11) 79%
> Define a function using range (11) 79%
> Perform basic operations on functions, including composition, long division, and inverse (11) 79%
> Apply the techniques of quadratic formula, factoring, and completing the square to solve quadratic equations (9) 64%
> Explore families of functions and recognize and graph various functions: Quadratic (9) 64%
> Explore families of functions and recognize and graph various functions: Exponential functions (9) 64%
> Solve a system of equations using matrices (9) 64%
> Define a function using inverse (8) 57%
> Explore families of functions and recognize and graph various functions: Polynomial (8) 57%
> Explore families of functions and recognize and graph various functions: Linear (8) 57%
> Solve absolute value inequalities and equations (8) 57%
> Solve applied problems using functions (8) 57%
> Solve quadratic inequalities (7) 50%
> Write equivalent forms of rational expressions and solve rational equalities and inequalities (7) 50%
> Distinguish between and use arithmetic and geometric sequences (6) 43%
> Distinguish between relations and functions (6) 43%
> Use function notation (6) 43%
> Simplify radical expressions and solve radical equations (6) 43%
> Solve problems using direct, inverse, combined, and joint variation (6) 43%
> Recognize, identify, and sketch graphs of a parabola, circle, ellipse, and hyperbola (6) 43%
> Find the nth term of a sequence (5) 36%
> Find the sum of a series (5) 36%
> Examine effects of parameters on a graph (5) 36%

Explore families of functions and recognize and graph various functions: Rational (5) 36%

Explore families of functions and recognize and graph various functions: Absolute value (5) 36%

Write a polynomial equation when given its roots (5) 36%

Identify conic equations using notions of translations (5) 36%

Use and prove simple laws of logarithms (5) 36%

Understand and use the inverse properties of logarithms and exponents (5) 36%

Apply trigonometry and geometry to real-world situations (5) 36%

Define a function using zeros (4) 29%

Explore families of functions and recognize and graph various functions (4) 29%

Explore families of functions and recognize and graph various functions: Step (4) 29%

Explore families of functions and recognize and graph various functions: Radical (4) 29%

Analyze functions and their properties (4) 29%

Use matrices to model and solves practical problems (4) 29%

Find the inverse of a matrix using a calculator (4) 29%

Solve linear programming problems (4) 29%

Recognize relationships among solutions, zeros, x-intercepts, and factors of a polynomial function or its graph (4) 29%

Prove and use trigonometry identities (4) 29%

Calculate the exact values of sine, cosine, and tangent for special angles of the unit circle (4) 29%

Data Analysis

Collect and analyze data (7) 50%

Find the equation of a curve of best fit (7) 50%

Make predictions using a regression equation (6) 43%

Develop mathematical models using functions (6) 43%

Investigate scatter plots for patterns (5) 36%

Make predictions, using data, scatter plots, or curve of best fit (5) 36%

Uses technology to find the line or curve of best fit for data collected (5) 36%

Analyze and synthesize data using measures of central tendency, dispersion, and shape (4) 29%

Probability

Calculate simple combinations and permutations of n objects taken r at a time (8) 57%

Calculate a probability using the fundamental counting principle (6) 43%

Computes simple, compound, and conditional probabilities (5) 36%

Comparison of Eleventh-Grade Precalculus Course Standards

The following comparisons involve standards for which at least 25 percent of the 11 states agreed.

Sequences

Work with recursive and closed formulas for arithmetic and geometric sequences and other functions (10) 91%

Use arithmetic sequences; find terms, formulas, sums (9) 82%

Use geometric sequences; find terms, formulas, sums (9) 82%

Work with infinite geometric series; find sum (9) 82%

Find sum of series (8) 73%
Solve exponential equations (7) 64%
Apply limits in problems of convergence and divergence (6) 55%
Solve logarithmic equations (6) 55%
Solve polynomial equations and inequalities (6) 55%
Use summation and factorial notation (3) 27%

Functions

Graph, analyze, and apply conic sections, including parabolas, hyperbolas, ellipses, circles, and degenerate conics (10) 91%
Analyze the graphs of the following functions: Rational (9) 82%
Analyze the graphs of the following functions: Logarithmic (8) 73%
Analyze the graphs of the following functions: Exponential (8) 73%
Find limits of functions at specific values and at infinity (8) 73%
Analyze functions with the following: Domain and range (7) 64%
Analyze functions with the following: Asymptotes (7) 64%
Use compositions and inverses (7) 64%
Use vectors to model and solve problems (7) 64%
Analyze functions with the following: Classification as continuous or discontinuous (6) 55%
Translate and transform functions (including nonlinear) (6) 55%
Use functions to model and solve problems (6) 55%
Use parametric equations to represent situations and functions (6) 55%
Solve trigonometric equations and inequalities using sum, difference, and both half- and double-angle formulas (6) 55%
Perform and analyze vector operations of addition, scalar multiplication, absolute value, and dot product (6) 55%
Plot and analyze properties of complex numbers in rectangular and polar coordinates (6) 55%
Analyze the graphs of the following functions: Trigonometric (5) 45%
Analyze the graphs of the following functions: Polynomial (5) 45%
Analyze functions with the following: Classification as increasing or decreasing (5) 45%
Describe fundamental characteristics of functions: End behavior (5) 45%
Verify trigonometric identities (5) 45%
Use the principle of mathematical induction as a form of proof (5) 45%
Analyze the graphs of the following functions: Piecewise-defined (4) 36%
Graph step functions (4) 36%
Analyze effects of parameter changes on graphs of functions (including trigonometric) (4) 36%
Relate symmetry to the behavior of even and odd functions (4) 36%
Describe fundamental characteristics of functions: Zeros (4) 36%
Apply the laws of sines and cosines (4) 36%
Use polar equations to model and solve problems (4) 36%
Convert coordinates, equations, and complex numbers in Cartesian form to polar form and vice versa (4) 36%
Apply the laws of logarithms (3) 27%
Relate and use degree and radian measure (3) 27%

Graph and evaluate trigonometric inverses (3) 27%
Work with operations, powers, roots, and absolute values of complex numbers (3) 27%
Determine average and instantaneous rates of change (3) 27%
Explore and interpret slopes of secants approaching slopes of tangents (3) 27%

Data Analysis

Fit and models linear and nonlinear curves to data (7) 64%

Probability

Use the binomial theorem (6) 55%

13

Grade 12: Process and Standards—Grades 9–12, Probability and Statistics

Michael Koehler, Chair; *Kansas City, Missouri*
Martha Aliaga, *American Statistical Association*
Tracy Newell, *Kansas State Department of Education*
Frank Quinn, *Virginia Polytechnic Institute*
Robert Riehs, *New Jersey Department of Education*

Process

The group looked at all states that had appropriate standards, either probability and statistics or Grades 9–12 combined

The Grade 12 team examined one content strand at a time, completing the review of that strand for all the relevant states before going on to another strand. Each member of the Grade 12 team took a single state document (or, in the case of very sparse state expectations, two state documents). As a group, the team discussed each learning expectation on the template and searched within state documents for learning expectations noted on the template. As individual team members located expectations, they read them aloud so that a group decision could be made as to whether the expectation matched a template item. After reviewing the expectations already listed on the coding sheets, individual team members then read aloud any additional state expectations that had not already been incorporated into the coding process. In this way, additional expectations were added to the coding chart, and some of the existing coding language was broadened to accommodate individual state expectations. This group coding process was repeated 3 or 4 times, for each strand, to accommodate review of all the relevant states. After all state documents were coded for one strand, another strand was chosen to review. Throughout this process, some expectations from the template were later found in unanticipated places in state documents. On such occasions, the expectations were encoded appropriately under previously reviewed strands on the templates.

Reader Reliability

The reader reliability rating for the Grade 12 team showed agreement on 13 out of 16 items tested (81%). Of the 13, five had to go to discussion before agreement was reached.

Trends from Grade 12

Few trends were found for Grade 12 mathematics. Overall, there were states with graduation requirements of varying types and some states with statistics and probability, or similar titled courses, and advanced placement courses. Most states that listed advanced placement courses simply specified the standards of those courses recommended as advanced placement; those are not included in this document.

Comparison of Grades 9–12 Standards (or Graduation Standards)

The set of standards for which at least 25 percent of the 21 states agreed follows:

Number

Identify and describe differences among number sets (14) 67%

Identify and describe differences among the following sets: Rational numbers (14) 67%

Identify and describe differences among the following sets: Natural numbers (13) 62%

Identify and describe differences among the following sets: Whole numbers (13) 62%

Identify and describe differences among the following sets: Integers (13) 62%

Identify and describe differences among the following sets: Irrational numbers (13) 62%

Evaluate and write numerical expressions involving integer exponents (13) 62%

Demonstrate computational fluency with all rational numbers (12) 57%

Recognize, describe, and use properties of the real number system (11) 52%

Apply properties of exponents to simplify expressions or solve equations (10) 48%

Judge the reasonableness of numerical computations and their results (9) 43%

Understand complex numbers (9) 43%

Compare, order, and determine equivalent forms for rational and irrational numbers (8) 38%

Apply scientific notation to perform computations, solve problems, and write representations of numbers (8) 38%

Evaluate expressions involving noninteger exponents (8) 38%

Add and subtract real numbers using powers and roots (8) 38%

Solve problems using simple matrix operations (including inverses) (8) 38%

Order of operations and simplification of numeric expressions (8) 38%

Simplify and perform basic operations on numerical expressions involving radicals (7) 33%

Distinguish between an exact and an approximate answer and recognize errors (6) 29%

Compare subsets of the real number system with regard to their properties: Commutative (6) 29%

Select among mental computation, paper-and-pencil calculations, or technology as needed (6) 29%

Select, convert, and apply an equivalent representation of a number for a specified situation (6) 29%

Organize problem situations using matrices (6) 29%

Compute with complex numbers (6) 29%

Measurement

Solve problems using indirect measurement (15) 71%

Determine linear measures, areas, and volumes (15) 71%

Use right triangle trigonometry to solve problems (13) 62%

Evaluate measurements for accuracy, precision, and error (11) 52%

Determine appropriate units and scales to use when solving measurement problems (10) 48%

Use the ratio of lengths in similar 2- or 3-dimensional figures to calculate the ratio of areas or volumes (9) 43%

Measure perimeter, weight, area, volume, temperature, angle, and distance using standard and nonstandard units (8) 38%

Use estimation to solve problems and to check accuracy of solutions (6) 29%

Algebra

Solve linear equations or inequalities (17) 81%

Interpret and solve systems of linear equations using graphing, substitution, elimination, and matrices using technology (17) 81%

Model real-world problems using functions (17) 81%

Translate among tabular, graphical, and algebraic representations of functions (16) 76%

Evaluate algebraic manipulation operations (11) 52%

Graph and interpret linear inequalities in one or two variables and systems of linear inequalities (11) 52%

Identify the domain and range of functions (11) 52%

Model real-life situations using linear expressions, equations, and inequalities (10) 48%

Determine if a relation is a function (9) 43%

Solve quadratic equations (8) 38%

Relate the effect of transformations on graphs and equations (8) 38%

Factor simple quadratics (8) 38%

Generalize patterns using functions or relationships (7) 33%

Explain how the graph of a linear function changes as the coefficients or constants are changed (7) 33%

Solve absolute value equations and inequalities (7) 33%

Identify, graph, and describe graphs of basic families of functions (7) 33%

Identify independent and dependent variables (6) 29%

Perform computation with polynomials (6) 29%

Use function notation (6) 29%

Identify, graph, and describe graphs of basic families of functions: Linear (6) 29%

Identify, graph, and describe graphs of basic families of functions: Absolute value (6) 29%

Identify, graph, and describe graphs of basic families of functions: Quadratic (6) 29%

Geometry

Formally define and explain key aspects of geometric figures (15) 71%

Perform translations and line reflections on the coordinate plane (14) 67%

Find perimeter, area, and volume (14) 67%

Apply proportions and right triangle trigonometric ratios to solve problems (13) 62%

Apply the Pythagorean theorem (12) 57%

Use inductive and deductive reasoning to establish the validity of geometric conjectures (11) 52%

Solve problems using congruence (11) 52%

Use transformations to demonstrate geometric properties (11) 52%

Define basic trigonometric ratios in right triangles (10) 48%

Make, test, and establish the validity of conjectures (10) 48%

Solve problems involving similarity (10) 48%

Analyze quadrilateral for defining characteristics (8) 38%

Calculate distance, midpoint coordinates, and slope (8) 38%

Graph a line when the slope and a point or when 2 points are known (7) 33%

Construct geometric figures using dynamic geometry software (6) 29%

Solve problems involving parts of the same circle (6) 29%

Describe and apply properties of polygons (6) 29%

Create 2-dimensional representations of 3-dimensional objects (6) 29%

       Use coordinate geometry to graph linear equations, determine slopes of lines, identify parallel and perpendicular lines (6) 29%

       Solve problems using vectors (6) 29%

Data Analysis

       Organize data using graphs (15) 71%

       Calculate combinations (14) 67%

       Create a scatter plot for a set of bivariate data, sketch the line of best fit, and interpret the slope of the line of best fit (11) 52%

       Calculate permutations (11) 52%

       Draw inferences from collections of data (11) 52%

       Determine the line of best fit and use it to predict (11) 52%

       Compute frequency, mean, median, mode, and range (10) 48%

       Design and conduct a statistical experiment (10) 48%

       Display a scatter plot, describe its shape, and determine regression coefficients, regression equations, and correlation coefficients of bivariate data (9) 43%

       Describe characteristics and limitations of sampling methods and analyze the effects of random versus biased sampling (8) 38%

       Formulate questions, design studies, and collect data about a characteristic (8) 38%

       Understand and compute variance and standard deviation (8) 38%

       Determine the most appropriate measure of central tendency for a set of data based on its distribution (7) 33%

       Given one-variable quantitative data, display the distribution, describe its shape, and calculate summary statistics (7) 33%

       Evaluate survey results (7) 33%

       Determine appropriate designs for experiments (6) 29%

Probability

       Use experimental or theoretical probability to solve problems (10) 48%

       Find and compare experimental and theoretical probability for a simple situation (10) 48%

       Solve problems involving dependent and independent events (8) 38%

       Compute probabilities using basic counting techniques, such as combinations and permutations (7) 33%

       Design, conduct, analyze, and communicate the results of probability experiments (7) 33%

       Use simulations to estimate probabilities (6) 29%

       Define probability in terms of sample spaces, outcome, events, and relative frequency (6) 29%

       Describe the concepts of conditional probability (6) 29%

Comparison of Twelfth-Grade Probability and Statistics Course Standards

There are six states that included a set of standards for a probability and statistics or a statistics course independent of other course work at that grade. Whereas some states had course expectations (standards), it was not clear that students had to take the courses. In other words, as in other courses for secondary school, the compared standards may not be for all students. Some states included the advanced placement syllabus in this category did not include separate standards. The first group is the set of standards for which at least 2 of the 6 states agreed.

Statistics

    Know the definitions of the mean, median, and mode of a distribution (6) 100%

    Use least squares regression to find the equation of line of best fit (6) 100%

    Use standard distributions: Normal (5) 83%

    Apply statistics in decision-making and hypothesis testing (5) 83%

    Calculate a correlation coefficient (5) 83%

    Design a survey instrument (5) 83%

    Organize and describe distributions of data by using histograms (4) 67%

    Compute the variance and standard deviation of a distribution of data (4) 67%

    Collect, read, and analyze data from real world (4) 67%

    Determine the sampling process and effects of sampling on outcomes (4) 67%

    Calculate z-scores, t-test, t-scores, quartiles, and ranges and explain their meaning (4) 67%

    Identify the central tendency and spread of data (4) 67%

    Explain how a correlation coefficient measures association (4) 67%

    Identify biased sampling methods (4) 67%

    Organize and describe distributions of data by using scatter plots (3) 50%

    Organize and describe distributions of data by using box-and-whisker plots (3) 50%

    Use standard distributions: Binomial (3) 50%

    Apply a logarithmic transformation to data (3) 50%

    Apply a power transformation to data (3) 50%

    Describe simple random sampling (3) 50%

    Plan a survey to answer a question (3) 50%

    Organize and describe distributions of data by using stem-and-leaf displays (2) 33%

    Use curve fitting to predict from collected data (2) 33%

    Defend regression models using correlation coefficients (2) 33%

    Design, execute, make conclusions, and communicate the results of a statistical experiment (2) 33%

    Examine graphs of data for outliers (2) 33%

    Compare two or more sets of univariate data by analyzing measures of center and spread (2) 33%

    Use regression lines to make predictions (2) 33%

    Use residual plots to determine if a linear model is satisfactory to describe the relationship between two variables (2) 33%

Probability

    Apply the counting principles, including permutations and combinations (5) 83%

    Construct confidence intervals to estimate a population parameter (5) 83%

    Interpret confidence intervals (5) 83%

    Describe and use the central limit theorem (5) 83%

    Develop binomial probability distributions (4) 67%

    Identify properties of a normal probability distribution (4) 67%

    Use a chi-square test (4) 67%

    Know the definition of independent events (3) 50%

    Explain the relationship between theoretical and experimental probability (3) 50%

Identify types of events, including mutually exclusive, independent, and complementary (3) 50%

Use the rules of addition and multiplication for probabilities (2) 33%

Know and use conditional probabilities (2) 33%

Understand the notion of discrete random variables and use them to solve for probabilities of outcomes (2) 33%

Use Markov chains to calculate probability by constructing matrix models (2) 33%

Limitations of the Study

Participants in the work in Park City were asked to list any limitations that needed to be noted in the final report document. The following limitations have been summarized to include those limitations. Additional limitations were added on the basis of the overall analysis of the work. The limitations are categorized to aid the reader.

Lack of Comparable Standards

Not all states have standards in all areas. This was a common concern for the readers of the standards for Grades 9–12. For example, one reviewer wrote, "Only a few states had actual Grade 11 standards."

Among the biggest concerns of the overall group were the many inconsistencies in the standards themselves. The intended audience was not always clear. Participants also questioned whether the latest and most complete standards documents were being used, although project codirectors had made every effort to provide the most recent and complete state-approved documents. The ASSM codirector contacted every state to try to determine if the correct documents were being used; during the Park City meeting, newer versions of three sets of documents were identified and given to the participants.

One participant expressed the concern that the introductory sections of state standards documents were not used, and those sections might have given more directions about standards in a given state.

Interpreting the Standards

Participants found that language from document to document left much to the interpretation of reviewers. In a number of states, they reported having to "interpret" the standards, which could have led to errors in coding. Most participants agreed that deciphering terminology in the standards was difficult.

That different groups worked separately on different grades may lead to inconsistency in accuracy of the final report of commonalities among the standards. When trying to code the standards, the final coded template might have included partial standards.

Because some states use a large grain size for standards, whereas others use a very small grain size, there are concerns about the accuracy of the results.

Additionally, standards rarely mentioned whether topics were to be learned only with a calculator, only without a calculator, or with and without a calculator. If no mention was made, then the interpretation was that no calculator was allowed.

Examination of Process Standards

Process standards are typically those that have been identified in NCTM's *Principles and Standards for School Mathematics* (2000). Those process standards are the following: problem solving, reasoning and proof, communication, connections, and representation. Process standards tend to be interwoven with the content standards and were only examined in those states that offered them as separate strands. One reviewer remarked, "It is possible that 'lines' [standards] were missed because the state 'hid' a concept in a different strand than expected [unique location]." Another participant wrote, "Overall, I think many states have similarities that were difficult to discover because of the wording used by states."

Need for More Time

A major concern from most of the participants was that the task was enormous. Participants noted that the task was monumental and there was a short amount of time in which to do the work.

In relation to the time issue, some concern existed that the templates provided for use to help the process may have been relied on too much and could have become the "standard" instead of an aid to help the process.

Validity and Reliability of the Process

Participants expressed concern about the process, and almost all worried about the validity and reliability of the process across grade levels. One person wrote, "We now know how reliable the groups' work is, in and of each group. However, it needs to be pointed out that this level of reliability cannot be extended when comparing between the grades. This was, basically, committee work and will suffer the same limitations as any final document that was compiled by committees that did not work together."

Concern for the Grades 9–12 Standards Work

Little consistency exists among standards for Grades 9–12. Some have individual grade-band standards; yet others have standards for named courses. As a result, the Grades 9–12 report uses data from only a limited number of reports. As a result of the inconsistencies in how the standards are written, some states might have standards that were missed.

Conclusions

In writing conclusions about the comparison of state standards, participants were asked to reflect on several questions as they considered the work in which they participated in Park City. Questions for reflection included the following:

1. From your perspective, what are characteristics of the most informative state standards that you have seen in this work?
2. From your perspective, what are characteristics of the least informative state standards you have seen?
3. If standards are to be understandable and usable to the mathematics community, what changes do you see as needed?
4. If standards are to be understandable to the public, what changes do you see as needed?

Each question is considered here in turn:

From your perspective, what are characteristics of the most informative state standards that you have seen in this work?

Participants noted the work of 24 states in this category. No single state had more than 5 nominations as the best. Thus, although participants arrived at no consensus on which state, or states, have exemplary standards, the following characteristics of state standards were noted as being exemplary:
• Use of a finer grain size for explication of the standards
• Use of a more general grain size for the standards
• Use of clear language
• Use of examples
• Focus on "big ideas" of what students need to learn
• Alignment with *Principles and Standards* (NCTM, 2000)

Most participants noted that the answer to this question might depend on the audience for the standards and the intended use. The answer may even depend on the grade level. The only definitive answer was that participants wanted the standards to be clear, well written, and mathematically accurate.

From your perspective, what are characteristics of the least informative state standards you have seen?

As participants answered this question, they mentioned explicitly 14 states that had characteristics of uninformative standards. Of those 14 states, 8 also were in the list of states as having the best standards. Only 2 states were singled out by 6 people as having only the least informative standards. Aspects of the standards that are least informative are the following:
• Use of incorrect or imprecise mathematical language
• Use of nonsubstantial content
• Use of broad or vague language
• Use of too many standards
• Use of language that is too wordy
• Use of grade bands instead of grade levels
• Use of multiple objectives in single statements
• Use of meaningless verbs or stock phrases, such as "appropriate methods"

• Use of repeated standards
• Use of multiple layers of standards (e.g., standards, objectives, benchmarks, expectations, etc.)
    The participants, in general, appeared to want standards that were precise, relied on a few well-defined verbs, and described what students were expected to do at grade level with clarity and mathematical accuracy.

If standards are to be most understandable and usable to the mathematics community, what changes do you see as needed?
Participants were fairly definitive in terms of what would help standards to be more understandable and usable to the mathematics community. A summary of the changes needed follows:
• A high degree of content specificity
• Vertical and horizontal alignment across grade levels
• Development and consistent growth across grade levels
• Distinction between core standards and standards for college-bound students
• Greater specificity of content and a glossary of terms
• Clear definitions of the action verbs used in the standards
• Fewer standards with a focus on "big ideas"
• Reduced jargon with clear statements
• Specification of the intended audiences
• A view of assessments to correlate with standards
• Specific examples of mathematics problems
    In answer to this question, it was noted that professional development for teachers should address how to write standards. In addition, several people noted the need for communication both among neighboring states and across the nation in determining what standards are needed. One participant wrote, "National standards need to give some guidance as to big concepts that need to be addressed by grade rather than by cluster with an understanding that these are recommendations for states to consider—not absolutes. Many states want this guidance; the same as districts want guidance from the state level." At the very least, the use of a standard template with a prescribed set of strands across the nation would be helpful.

If standards are to be understandable to the public, what changes do you see as needed?
Whether the changes needed were for the mathematical community or for the public at large, similar recommendations were made. They are listed here both for emphasis and for consistency:
• Use of clear, precise language
• Use of correct and standard mathematical vocabulary and usage
• Use of examples of specific indicators
• Use of information that can be disseminated to PTO/PTA groups
• Parent involvement in standards review
• Use of glossary of mathematical words and terms
• Avoidance of brevity in the statement of the standards
• Avoidance of the use of the table of contents of a textbook as a framework for or statement of standards
• Use of statement of standards by grade level
• Organization of standards around big ideas
    Other expressed views included, "A separate document written for the layman a la the versions of the 1989 standards [*Curriculum and Evaluations Standards for School Mathematics* (NCTM, 1989)] that were created for different audiences." Yet others thought that this was not

possible beyond eighth grade because of the use of the mathematics language that must be involved. One participant wrote, "To me, we need a media PR campaign to target the general public on the highlights or core principles of our work. I know $ [dollars] can be a block to PR."

It is clear that there is consensus that all standards documents need to be clear and concise, written in mathematically correct language, and with a glossary of terms. From a practical standpoint, it is fairly clear that the glossary must be an appendix; otherwise, the length of the glossary may overwhelm the standards themselves. One concern is that the glossary could "become" the standards and again thwart the need to identify the "big ideas" of school mathematics.

Broad Conclusions

Most standards are designed to describe the desired learning for all students. This fact raises many questions in the design of standards at the high school level and makes it unclear what the expectations are for all students. Are the expectations the same for all for a graduation requirement? Are they different for college-intending students? Do the standards imply that all students should continue mathematics throughout their high school careers? If states have different expectations for different students, should those differing expectations be outlined? A disadvantage of outlining standards in that manner is that there may then become an issue of equity for students. Is the mathematics accessible to all students in an intellectually honest way?

Because tests and curricula typically follow the standards, there are issues regarding which tests and which curricula would need to be used for which students. As it now stands with most state standards, the college-bound students and their teachers are given little guidance for student study. One participant's assertion, "My colleagues and I should write standards for courses for college-bound high school students," is not a common view of the participants. In fact, one of the real assets of the Park City work was that in this rare instance, both state supervisors and mathematicians made a concerted effort to see what the standards say and to consider how they might be improved.

A participant noted, "In spite of any negative features [of the Park City work], I believe that depending on the future use of its outcome, it could be an extremely important step in providing direction to national curriculum development. I knew coming into the project what many of the downsides might be, but I hope that they were more than overcome by the efforts of the group."

One outcome of the project is the identification of the need for more conversation among the variety of perspectives represented by the conference participants. The mix of mathematicians, mathematics educators and teachers, and state supervisors was healthy and provides a common understanding of many of the issues involved with writing a set of standards in mathematics. Among the recommendations that are worthy of consideration are the following:

- Development of a glossary of terms for state standards
  The development of this glossary might help add consistency to standards whether or not it is appended to the standards for each state.
- Differentiation of curriculum
  A conversation among participants of the type mentioned above should consider whether there should be differentiated curriculum at the high school level for college-intending and non-college-intending students.
- Examination of curricular standards vertically
  With the work that was done in 2004, it would be helpful to determine if there is some consistency in alignment of curriculum across the grades vertically. That type of consideration would make concrete suggestions about standards at grade level possible.

- Conversation to consider a national curriculum
  The work done at Park City sets the stage for a national discussion about the feasibility and desirability of a national curriculum. If we are serious about making a concerted effort to change and improve mathematics in the United States, a conversation dedicated to this topic is required. Such a conversation must actively involve mathematicians, scientists, teacher practitioners, mathematics and science educators, business members, and parents. A national curriculum is not a trivial undertaking and is a bigger topic than any single mathematics organization can direct.

References

Blank, Rolf. "Surveys of Enacted Curriculum Multi-purpose Tools for Alignment, Evaluation, Improving Instruction," 2003. Available from www.ccsso.org/sec/.

Blank, Rolf K., Andrew Porter, and S. Smithson. "New Tools for Analyzing Teaching, Curriculum and Standards in Mathematics and Science." Report from Survey of Enacted Curriculum Project (National Science Foundation REC98-03080). Washington, D.C.: Council of Chief State School Officers, 2001.

Bulletin IV. IEA, 1979, p. 19.

Council of Chief State School Officers (CCSSO) (2003). [http://www.ccsso.org/projects/State_Education_Indicators/Key_State_Education_Policies/3160.cfm#I]

Floden, Robert. E., Andrew C. Porter, William H. Schmidt, D. J. Freeman, and J. R. Schwille. "Responses to Curriculum Pressures: A Policy Capturing Study of Teacher Decisions about Content." *Journal of Educational Psychology* 73 (1981): 129–41.

Hirstein, James. "From Royaumont to Bielefeld: A Twenty-Year Cross-National Survey of the Content of School Mathematics." In *Comparative Studies of Mathematics Curricula: Change and Stability 1960-1980*. Proceedings of a conference jointly organized by the Institute for the Didactics of Mathematics (IDM) and the International Mathematics Committee of the Second International Mathematics Study of the International Association for the Evaluation of Educational Achievement (IEA). Osnabruck, Germany: Institut fur Didaktik der Matehmatik der Universitat Bielefeld, 1980.

National Council of Teachers of Mathematics. *Curriculum and Evaluation Standards for School Mathematics*. Reston, Va.: National Council of Teachers of Mathematics, 1989.

———. *Principles and Standards for School Mathematics*. Reston, Va.: National Council of Teachers of Mathematics, 2000.

Porter, Andrew C. "2002 Presidential Address: Measuring the Content of Instruction: Uses in Research and Practice." *Educational Researcher* 31 (July 2002): 3–14.

Raimi, Ralph A., and L. S. Braden. "State Mathematics Standards: An Appraisal of Math Standards in 46 States, the District of Columbia, and Japan." Fordham Report, Vol. 2, No. 3, March 1998. Available from http://www.edexcellence.net/standards/math/math.htm.

Schmidt, William. 2003. Available from http://www.ed.gov/inits/mathscience/schmidt.html.

Schmidt, William H., Curtis C. McKnight, and Senta Raizen. *A Splintered Vision: An Investigation of U.S. Science and Mathematics Education*. Dordrecht, Netherlands: Kluwer, 1997.

Stigler, James W., and James Hiebert. *The TIMSS Videotape Classroom Study.* Washington, D.C.: National Center for Education Statistics, 1997.

Webb, Norman L. *Alignment of Science and Mathematics Education Standards and Assessments in Four States* (Research Monograph No. 18). Madison, Wis.: University of Wisconsin—Madison, National Institute for Science Education, 1999.

U.S. Department of Education. "Testing for Results." Available from www.ed.gov/nclb/accountability/ayp/testingforresults.html

Appendix I: Participants

ASSM/NCTM National Math View Participants
Park City, Utah
July 21–25, 2004

Claudia L. Ahlstrom
Mathematics Consultant
New Mexico Public Education
Department
300 Don Gasper
Santa Fe, NM 87501

Martha Aliaga
2121 Jamieson Avenue #1209
Alexandria, VA 22314

Carolyn L. Baldree
Program Specialist-Mathematics
Georgia Department of Education
1754 Twin Towers East
Atlanta, GA. 30334-5040

Ann Bartosh
Mathematics Consultant
Kentucky Department of Education
500 Mero Street, 18th floor
Frankfort, KY 40601

Hyman Bass
Department of Mathematics
University of Michigan
3864 East Hall
525 East University
Ann Arbor, MI 48109

Jennie M. Bennett
5422 Bythewood Street
Houston, TX 77021

Wesley L. Bird (President, ASSM)
Director, Curriculum and Technology
Integration
Department of Elementary and
Secondary Education
P.O. Box 480
Jefferson City, MO 65102-0480

Deborah Kiger Bliss
Mathematics Specialist

Secondary Instructional Services
Virginia Department of Education
P. O. Box 2120
Richmond, VA 23218

Margaret (Peg) Bondorew
42 Pierce Street
Foxboro, MA 02035

Laurie Boswell
1484 Coppermine Road
Monroe, NH 03771

David Brancamp
Nevada Department of Education
700 East Fifth Street, Suite 108
Carson City, Nevada 89701

Glenn Bruckhart
1149 Ridge Road
Littleton, CO 80120

Cynthia G. Bryant
28 Magnolia Drive
Salem, MO 65560

Sally Caldwell
Delaware Department of Education
P. O. Box 1402, Townsend Building
Dover, DE 19903-1402

Herb Clemens
Director, Park City Mathematics
Institute
Department of Mathematics
Ohio State University
231 West 18th Avenue
Columbus, OH 43210

Jerry Dancis
Department of Mathematics
University of Maryland
College Park, MD 20742

David M. DeCoste
4 Archibald Court
Antigonish, Nova Scotia B2G2V6,
CANADA

Dan Dolan
6 Shadow Lane
Cromwell, CT 06416

Jerry Dwyer
Department of Mathematics
Texas Tech University
Lubbock, TX 79409

Scott Eddins
Mathematics Coordinator
Tennessee Department of Education
Andrew Johnson Tower, 5th Floor
Nashville, TN 37243-0379

Gail R. Englert
School of International Studies at
Meadowbrook
239 Duke Street, Unit 307
Norfolk, VA 23510

Jerry L. Evans
Curriculum Specialist, Secondary
Mathematics
Utah State Office of Education
P. O. Box 144200
Salt Lake City, UT 84114-4200

Kaye Forgione
8209 Gutherie Drive
Austin, TX 78750

Trecina H. Green
Mississippi Department of Education
359 North West Street
P. O. Box 771
Jackson, MS 39205-0771

Linda D. Hackett
514 Clagett Street SW
Leesburg, VA 20175

Bonnie J. Hagelberger

5005 Archer Lane North
Plymouth, MN 55446

M. Kathleen Heid
2465 Circleville Road, Unit 102
State College, PA 16803

David Hoff
1034 Ohmer Street
Bottineau, ND 58318

Roger Howe
Department of Mathematics
Yale University
P.O. Box 208283
New Haven, CT 06520

Dan Hupp
77 Lewis Road
Newcastle, ME 04553

Susan J. Iida
200 P Street, Unit D-34
Sacramento, CA 95814

Rick Jennings
Mathematics Program Supervisor
Washington State Office of the
Superintendent of Public Instruction
P.O. Box 47200
Olympia, WA 98504-7200

Jeane M. Joyner
3021 Eton Road
Raleigh, NC 27608

Robert Kansky
1191 Granite Springs Road, Lot 10
Cheyenne, WY 82009

Diana Kasbaum
Mathematics Consultant, Successful
Schools Team
Wisconsin Department of Public
Instruction
125 South Webster Street
P.O. Box 7841
Madison, WI 53707-7841

Judith (Judi) Keeley
Rhode Island Department of Education
255 Westminster Street
Providence, RI 02903

Robert (Bob) W. Kenney
26 Wildwood Drive
Burlington, VT 05401

Michael Kestner
U.S. Department of Education
OESE/Mathematics and Science
Partnership
FB-6, Room 5C149
400 Maryland Avenue
Washington, DC 20202-6200

Harvey Keynes
School of Mathematics
University of Minnesota
127 Vincent
206 Church Street East, SE
Minneapolis, MN 55455

Mike Koehler
1228 West 72nd Street
Kansas City, MO 64114

Johnny W. Lott
Codirector, National Math View
Department of Mathematical Sciences
University of Montana
Missoula, MT 59812

Andy Magid
Department of Mathematics
University of Oklahoma
Norman, OK 73019

Frank Marburger
665 Bullfrog Valley Road
Hummelstown, PA 17036

Sarah F. Mason
Mathematics Specialist
Alabama Department of Education

3345 Gordon Persons Building
P.O. Box 302101
Montgomery, AL 36130

William McCallum
5130 North Campbell Avenue
Tucson, AZ 85718

Toni Meyer
Mathematics Consultant
NC Dept of Public Instruction
301 N. Wilmington Street
Raleigh, NC 27601-2825

Anne M. Mikesell
Mathematics Consultant
Ohio Department of Education
25 S. Front Street, Mailstop 509
Columbus, OH 43215-4183

Paula S. Moeller
Director of Mathematics
Texas Education Agency
1701 N. Congress Avenue
Austin, TX 78701-1494

Barbara Montalto
9002 Talleyran Drive
Austin, TX 78750

Kathy Mowers
Owensboro Community and Technical
College
4800 New Hartford Road
Owensboro, KY 42303

Mari Muri
6 Shadow Lane
Cromwell, CT 06416

Tracy Newell
KSDE Mathematics Consultant
120 SE 10th Avenue
Topeka, KS 66612-1182

Kathleen R. Nishimura
Codirector, National Math View

Hawaii State Department of Education
475 22nd Avenue, Room 116
Honolulu, HI 96816

Mattye Pollard-Cole
5765 East Long Place
Centennial, CO 80112

Frank Quinn
Department of Mathematics
Virginia Polytechnic Institute
Blacksburg, VA 24061

Barbara J. Reys
303 Townsend Hall
University of Missouri
Columbia, MO 65211

Robert J. Riehs
2134 Cloverly Hill Road
Broomall, PA 19008

Michael Roach
Mathematics Consultant
Indiana Department of Education
Room 229, State House
Indianapolis, IN 46204-2798

Bob D. Robinson
8707A 1st Place, NE
Everett, WA 98205

James M. Rubillo
Executive Director
NCTM
1906 Association Drive
Reston, VA 20191

Mary Ruzga
521 Cambridge Drive
Spartanburg, SC 29301

Diane L. Schaefer
Director, Office of Instruction
Rhode Island Department of Education
255 Westminster Street
Providence, RI 02903-3400

Anthony Mthomba Scott
1624 N. Nashville Avenue
Chicago, IL 60707

Cathy Seeley
President, NCTM
4907 Placid Place
Austin, TX 78731
Phone: 512-374-9777
Email: cseeley@nctm.org

Richard (Dick) T. Seitz
401 North Montana Avenue
Helena, MT 59601

Carolyn Sessions
Louisiana Dept of Education
1201 North 3rd Street, Room 4-211
Baton Rouge, LA 70802

Nanci Spear
PO Box 35155
Juneau, AK 99803

Barbara Stewart
6531 East Swamp Road
Conesus, NY 14435

Donna Taylor
Consultant Title II-A
NC DPI
6330 Mail Service Center
Raleigh NC 27699-6330

Sue White
905 6th Street SW Apt. 808-B
Washington, DC 20024

Lois Williams
Middle School Mathematics Specialist
P.O. Box 2120
James Monroe Building/20th Floor
Richmond, VA 23218

W. Stephen Wilson
Department of Mathematics
Johns Hopkins University
Baltimore, MD 21218

There were two participants who requested not to be listed.

Appendix II: Summary of State Mathematics Grade-Level Documents

Table 1: Summary of State Mathematics Grade-Level Expectation (GLE) Documents (What states have GLEs? What grades are included?)

Elementary/Middle School Grade-Level Expectations (GLEs)			High School Learning Expectations (LEs)		
Grade level (K–8)	Grade level (K–7; 2–8; 3–8; or 3–10)	No GLEs	Grade band (9–10; 11–12; HS; 9–12; or Graduation)	Course LEs	No LEs
AL, AZ, AR, CO, FL, GA, HI, ID, IN, KS, LA, MD, MI, MN, MS, MO, NC, NH, NV, NM, ND, OH, OK, OR, RI, SC, SD, TN, TX, VT, VA, WA, WV, WY, DC, DoDEA	AK – 3–10 CA – K–7 MT – 3–10 NJ – 3–8 UT – K–7	DE, IL, IA, KY, MA, ME, NE, NY, PA, WI	AK, AZ, CO, CT, ID, KS, LA, MN, MO, MT, NV, NJ, NM, ND, OH, SC, SD, VT, WA, WY, WI	AL, CA, GA, HI, IN, MD, MS, NC, OK, TN, TX, UT, VA, WV	AR, DE, FL, IL, IA, KY, ME, MA, MI, NE, NH, NY, OR, PA, RI
37	5	10	20	14	16

Data primarily from the Center for the Study of Mathematics Curriculum; Dr. Barbara Reys, director; funded by the National Science Foundation under the Center for Learning and Teaching Program, 2004

Dates for the available GLEs are shown in Table 2.

Table 2. Approval Dates of Grade Level Expectation Documents

Year	Number	States
2004	11	AK, GA, HI, MA, MI, MO, NH, ND, RI, VT, WA
2003	11	AL, AZ, KS, KY, LA, MD, MN, NC, UT, WV, WY
2002	6	ID, NJ, NM, OK, OR, VA
2001	3	NV, OH, TN
2000	5	CA, CO, IN, MS, SC
Pre-2000	13	AR, CT, DE, FL, IL, ME, MT, NE, NY, PA, SD, TX, WI

Data from Center for Learning and Teaching, University of Missouri—Columbia; Dr. Barbara Reys, Director, July 21, 2004.

Table 3 shows how fast the field is changing with GLE documents available in September 2004.

Table 3: Summary of State Grade Level Expectation (GLE) Documents

State	GLE Doc.	Year	Grades	Strands
Alabama	Yes	2003	K, 1, 2, 3, 4, 5, 6, 7, 8, algebra I, geometry, algebraic connections, algebra II, algebra II with trigonometry, algebra III with statistics, precalculus	Number and Operation; Algebra; Geometry; Measurement; Data Analysis and Probability
Alaska	Yes	2004	3, 4, 5, 6, 7, 8, 9, 10	Numeration; Measurement; Estimation and Computation; Functions and Relationships; Geometry; Statistics and Probability; Problem Solving; Communication; Reasoning; Connections
Arizona	Yes	2003	K, 1, 2, 3, 4, 5, 6, 7, 8, high school	Number Sense and Operation; Data Analysis; Probability and Discrete Mathematics; Patterns, Algebra, and Functions; Geometry and Measurement; Structure and Logic
Arkansas	Yes	1998	K, 1, 2, 3, 4, 5, 6, 7, 8	Numbers, Properties, and Operations; Geometry and Spatial Sense; Measurement; Data Analysis, Statistics, and Probability; Patterns, Algebra, and Functions

California	Yes	2000	K, 1, 2, 3, 4, 5, 6, 7, algebra I, geometry, algebra II, trigonometry, mathematical analysis, linear algebra, probability and statistics, AP probability and statistics, calculus	Number Sense; Algebra and Functions; Measurement and Geometry; Statistics, Data Analysis, and Probability; Mathematical Reasoning
Colorado	Yes	2000	3, 4, 5, 6, 7, 8, 9, 10	Number Sense; Algebra; Data Analysis, Probability, and Statistics; Geometry; Measurement; Computation
Connecticut	Yes	2004 Draft	PreK, K, 1, 2, 3, 4, 5, 6, 7, 8, 9–10, 11–12 Because only in draft form, not considered in the deliberations	Algebraic Reasoning: Patterns and Functions; Numerical and Proportional Reasoning; Geometry and Measurement; Working with Data
Delaware	No	1995	K–3, 4–5, 6–8, 9–10	Problem Solving; Communication; Reasoning; Connections; Estimation, Measurement, and Computation; Number Sense; Algebra; Spatial Sense and Geometry; Statistics and Probability; Patterns, Relationships, and Functions

District of Columbia	Yes	n/a	PreK, K, 1, 2, 3, 4, 5, 6, 7, 8, algebra I, geometry, algebra II, precalculus, AP calculus	Number and Operation; Patterns, Functions and Algebra; Data Analysis, Statistics, and Probability; Geometry and Spatial Sense; Measurement;
Florida	Yes	1996	K, 1, 2, 3, 4, 5, 6, 7, 8	Number Sense, Concepts, and Operations; Measurement; Geometry and Spatial Sense; Algebraic Thinking; Data Analysis and Probability
Georgia	Yes	2004	K, 1, 2, 3, 4, 5, 6, 7, 8, mathematics I, II, III, IV; foundations of math I, II, III, IV; high school accelerated mathematics I and II	Number and Operation; Algebra; Geometry; Measurement; Data Analysis and Probability; Process Skills
Hawaii	Yes	2004	K, 1, 2, 3, 4, 5, 6, 7, 8, pre-algebra, algebra I, algebra II, geometry, trigonometry, analytic geometry, probability, statistics, CPP-MM1, CPP-MM2, CPP-MM3, CPP-MM4, calculus	Number and Operation; Measurement; Geometry and Spatial Sense; Patterns, Functions, and Algebra; Data Analysis and Probability
Idaho	Yes	2002	K, 1, 2, 3, 4, 5, 6, 7, 8, 9–12	Basic Arithmetic, Estimation, and Accurate Computations; Mathematical Reasoning and Problem Solving; Concepts and Principles of Measurement; Concepts and

				Principles of Algebra; Concepts and Principles of Geometry; Data Analysis, Probability, and Statistics; Functions and Mathematical Modeling
Illinois	No	1997	Early elementary, late elementary, middle/junior high, early high school, late high school	Number Sense; Estimation and Measurement; Algebra and Analytical Methods; Geometry; Data Analysis and Probability
Indiana	Yes	2000	K, 1, 2, 3, 4, 5, 6, 7, 8, algebra I, algebra II, geometry, integrated math I, II, and III, precalculus, calculus, probability and statistics, discrete mathematics	Number Sense; Computation; Algebra and Functions; Geometry; Measurement; Data Analysis and Probability; Problem Solving
Iowa		n/a		
Kansas	Yes	2003	K, 1, 2, 3, 4, 5, 6, 7, 8, 9–10	Number and Computation; Algebra; Geometry; Data
Kentucky	Yes	2003	Primary–5, 6–8, 9–11 for core content; 3, 4, 6, 7 for vertically aligned core content (draft form)	Number and Computation; Geometry/ Measurement; Probability/ Statistics; Algebraic Ideas/Thinking
Louisiana	Yes	2003	PreK, K, 1, 2, 3, 4, 5, 6, 7, 8, 9, 10, 11–12	Number and Number Relations; Measurement; Algebra; Geometry; Data Analysis, Probability, and Discrete

				Mathematics; Patterns, Relations, and Functions
Maine	No	1997	PreK–2, 3–4, 5–8, secondary	Number and Number Sense; Computation; Data Analysis and Statistics; Probability; Geometry; Measurement; Patterns, Relations, Functions; Algebraic Concepts; Discrete Mathematics; Mathematical Reasoning; Mathematical Communication
Maryland	Yes	2003 (Draft)	PreK,K, 1, 2, 3, 4, 5, 6, 7, 8, algebra/data analysis, geometry	Algebra, Patterns and Functions; Geometry; Measurement; Statistics; Number Relationships and Computation; Problem Solving; Reasoning; Communication; Connections
Massachusetts	Yes	2000 and 2004	PreK–K, 1–2, 3–4, 5–6, 7–8, 9–10, 11–12, algebra I, geometry, algebra II, precalculus; specific standards developed in 2004 for 3, 5, 7	Number Sense and Operations; Patterns, Relations, and Algebra; Geometry; Measurement; Data Analysis, Statistics, and Probability
Michigan	Yes	2004	K, 1, 2, 3, 4, 5, 6, 7, 8	Number and Operation; Algebra; Measurement; Geometry; Data and Probability

Minnesota	Yes	2003	K, 1, 2, 3, 4, 5, 6, 7, 8, 9–11,11–12 (meant for flexibility)	Mathematical Reasoning; Number Sense, Computation, and Operations; Patterns, Functions, and Algebra; Data Analysis, Statistics, and Probability; Spatial Sense, Geometry, and Measurement
Mississippi	Yes	2000	K, 1, 2, 3, 4, 5, 6, 7, 8, pre-algebra, algebra I, geometry, algebra II, survey of mathematical topics, advanced algebra, precalculus, trigonometry, calculus, AP calculus, discrete mathematics, probability and statistics, AP statistics	Patterns/Algebraic Thinking; Data Analysis/ Prediction; Measurement; Geometric Concepts; Number Sense
Missouri	Yes	2004	K, 1, 2, 3, 4, 5, 6, 7, 8, 9, 10, 11, 12	Number and Operation; Algebraic Relationships; Geometry and Spatial Relationships; Measurement; Data and Probability
Montana	Yes	2003 (Draft)	3, 4, 5, 6, 7, 8, 10, graduation	No Strands
Nebraska	No	1998	K–1, 2–4, 5–8, 9–12	Numeration/ Number Sense; Computation/ Estimation; Measurement; Geometry/Spatial Concepts; Data Analysis, Probability and Statistical Concepts; Algebraic Concepts

Nevada	Yes	2001	K, 1, 2, 3, 4, 5, 6, 7, 8, 9–12	Numbers, Number Sense, and Computation; Patterns, Functions, and Algebra; Measurement; Spatial Relationships and Geometry; Data Analysis; Problem Solving; Mathematical Communication; Mathematical Reasoning; Mathematical Connections
New Hampshire	Yes	2004	K, 1, 2, 3, 4, 5, 6, 7, 8	Number and Operations; Geometry and Measurement; Functions and Algebra; Data, Statistics, and Probability
New Jersey	Yes	2002	K–2, 3, 4, 5, 6, 7, 8, 9–12	Numbers and Numerical Operations; Geometry and Measurement; Patterns and Algebra; Data Analysis, Probability, and Discrete Mathematics; Mathematical Processes
New Mexico	Yes	2002	K, 1, 2, 3, 4, 5, 6, 7, 8, 9–12	Numbers and Operations; Algebra; Geometry; Measurement; Data Analysis and Probability

New York	No	1999	PreK–K, 1–2, 3–4, 5–6, 7–8, math A, math B	Mathematical Reasoning; Number and Numeration; Operations; Modeling and Multiple Representation; Measurement; Uncertainty; Patterns/Functions
North Carolina	Yes	2003	K, 1, 2, 3, 4, 5, 6, 7, 8, introductory mathematics, algebra I, geometry, algebra II, technical mathematics I and II, advanced functions and modeling, discrete mathematics, precalculus, integrated mathematics 1,2,3, and 4, AP statistics, AP calculus	Number and Operation; Measurement; Geometry; Data Analysis and Probability; Algebra
North Dakota	Yes	2004 Draft	K, 1, 2, 3, 4, 5, 6, 7, 8, 9–10, 11–12	Number and Operation; Geometry and Spatial Sense; Data Analysis, Statistics, and Probability; Measurement; Algebra, Functions, and Patterns
Ohio	Yes	2001	K, 1, 2, 3, 4, 5, 6, 7, 8, 9, 10, 11, 12	Number, Number Sense, and Operations; Measurement; Geometry and Spatial Sense; Patterns, Functions, and Algebra; Data Analysis and Probability; Mathematical Processes
Oklahoma	Yes	2002	K, 1, 2, 3, 4, 5, 6, 7, 8, algebra I, algebra II, geometry	Patterns and Algebraic Reasoning; Number Sense; Number Operations and Computation;

				Geometry and Measurement; Data Analysis, Probability, and Statistics
Oregon	Yes	2002	K, 1, 2, 3, 4, 5, 6, 7, 8, CIM	Calculations and Estimations; Statistics and Probability; Algebraic Relationships; Measurement; Geometry; Mathematical Problem Solving
Pennsylvania	No	1999	3, 5, 8, 11	Numbers, Number Systems, and Number Relationships; Computation and Estimation; Measurement and Estimation; Mathematical Reasoning and Connections; Mathematical Problems Solving and Communication; Statistics and Data Analysis; Probability and Predictions; Algebra and Functions; Geometry; Trigonometry; Concepts of Calculus
Rhode Island	Yes	2004	K, 1, 2, 3, 4, 5, 6, 7, 8	Number and Operations; Geometry and Measurement; Functions and Algebra; Data,

				Statistics and Probability
South Carolina	Yes	2000	PreK, K, 1, 2, 3, 4, 5, 6, 7, 8, 9–12	Number and Operations, Algebra; Geometry; Measurement; Data Analysis
South Dakota	Yes	2004	K, 1, 2, 3, 4, 5, 6, 7, 8, 9–12	Algebra; Geometry; Measurement; Number Sense; Statistics and Probability
Tennessee	Yes	2001	K, 1, 2, 3, 4, 5, 6, 7, 8; different standards for high school courses: competency mathematics, foundations I and II, algebra I, geometry, algebra II, integrated mathematics I, II, and III, advanced algebra and trigonometry, discrete mathematics with statistics and probability, precalculus, statistics, calculus	Number and Operations; Algebra; Geometry; Measurement; Data Analysis and Probability
Texas	Yes	1998	K, 1, 2, 3, 4, 5, 6, 7, 8, algebra I, algebra II, geometry, precalculus, mathematical models with applications	Number, Operation, and Quantitative Reasoning; Patterns, Relationships, and Algebra; Geometry and Spatial Reasoning; Measurement; Probability and Statistics; Underlying Processes and Mathematical Tools
Utah	Yes	2003	K, 1, 2, 3, 4, 5, 6, math 7, prealgebra, elementary algebra, geometry, intermediate algebra, precalculus, calculus, statistics, applied mathematics I and II	Number Sense and Operations; Patterns, Relations, and Functions; Geometry and Spatial Relationships; Measurement; Data Analysis and

				Probability
Vermont	Yes	2004	K, 1, 2, 3, 4, 5, 6, 7, 8, high school	Arithmetic, Number, and Operation Concepts; Geometry and Measurement; Functions and Algebra; Data, Statistics, and Probability; Mathematical Dimensions; Mathematical Problem Solving; Communications; Applications
Virginia	Yes	2002	K, 1, 2, 3, 4, 5, 6, 7, 8, algebra I, algebra II, geometry, trigonometry, computer mathematics, probability and statistics, discrete mathematics, mathematical analysis	Number and Number Sense; Computation and Estimation; Measurement; Geometry; Probability and Statistics; Patterns, Functions, and Algebra
Washington	Yes	2004	K, 1, 2, 3, 4, 5, 6, 7, 8, 9–10	Number Sense; Measurement; Geometric Sense; Probability and Statistics; Algebraic Sense
West Virginia	Yes	2003	K, 1, 2, 3, 4, 5, 6, 7, 8, algebra/geometry preparation, algebra I, algebra II, applied mathematics I and II, geometry and applied geometry, conceptual mathematics, trigonometry, probability and statistics, precalculus	Number and Operations; Algebra; Geometry; Measurement; Data Analysis and Probability
Wisconsin	No	1998	4, 8, 12	Mathematical Processes; Number

				Operations and Relationships; Geometry; Measurement; Statistics and Probability; Algebraic Relationships
Wyoming	Yes	2003	K, 1, 2, 3, 4, 5, 6, 7, 8, 9–12 (stated as Grade 11)	Number Operations and Concepts; Geometry; Measurement; Algebraic Concepts and Relationships; Data Analysis and Probability

Prepared by the staff of the Center for the Study of Mathematics Curriculum, University of Missouri, Dr. Barbara Reys, Director (http://mathcurriculumcenter.org); September 2004

Appendix III: Example of the Original Template

Grade 5	
Strand	
Number	
Number Sense	Read, write, or represent decimals using symbols, words, or models
	Identify irrational numbers and locate them relative to other numbers
	Read, write, or represent fractions or mixed numbers using symbols, models, and words
	Identify or determine equivalent forms of proper fractions
	Explain different interpretations of fractions: as parts of a whole, parts of a set, and division of whole numbers by whole numbers
	Understand the relative magnitude of ones, tenths, and hundredths and the relationship of each place value to the place to its right
	Identify numbers less than zero by extending the number line
	Reads, writes, and identifies common percents
	Understand percentages as parts out of 100, use % notation, and express a part of a whole as a percentage
	Interpret percents as a part of a hundred; find decimal and percent equivalents for common fractions and explain why they represent the same value
	Compare, order, round, and expand whole numbers through millions and decimals to thousandths
	Compare or order fractions with or without using the symbols (<, >, or =)
	Compare two whole numbers, fractions, and decimals
	Compare, order, or describe decimals with or without using the symbols (<, >, or =)
	Compare and order positive and negative integers
	Identify on a number line the relative position of simple positive fractions, positive mixed numbers, and positive decimals
	Change mixed numbers to improper fractions
	Determine the equivalency between and among fractions, decimals, and percents in contextual situations
	Express ratios in several ways given applied situations recognize and find equivalent ratios
	Reduce fractions to lowest terms
	Recognize that 1 is neither prime nor composite
Number Theory	Identify or describe numbers as prime or composite

		Identify and use rules of divisibility for 2, 3, 4, 5, 6, 9, 10
		Identify the greatest common factor
		Identify a common multiple and the least common multiple
		Find the prime factorization of numbers between 1 and 50, express in exponential notation, and understand that every whole number can be expressed as a product of primes
	Number Operation/ Computation	Demonstrate computational fluency with addition, subtraction, multiplication, and division of whole numbers
		Multiply two-digit numbers by two-digit numbers
		Divide three-digit numbers by a single digit
		Add and subtract fractions (including mixed numbers) with different denominators
		Add and subtract fractions with like denominators
		Use models to show an understanding of multiplication and division of fractions
		Multiply and divide fractions to solve problems
		Use mental arithmetic to add or subtract simple decimals
		Add and subtract decimals and verify the reasonableness of the results
		Demonstrate the distributive property of multiplication over addition
		Identify such properties as commutativity, associativity, and distributivity and use them to compute with whole numbers
	Estimation	Use estimation to verify the reasonableness of a calculation
		Round to estimate quantities
		Determine from real-world problems whether an estimated or exact answer is acceptable
Measurement		
	Measurement Tools/Scales	Read customary and metric measurement scales
		Measure in customary and metric units
		Estimate and determine weight
		Estimate and determine capacity
		Select and use appropriate tools and units
		Draw 2-dimensional figures to specifications using the appropriate tools
		Measure angles
		Convert measurement units to equivalent units within a given system (U.S. customary and metric)
		Differentiate between, and use appropriate units of measures for, two- and three-dimensional objects (i.e., find the perimeter, area, volume)

Perimeter, Area, and Volume	Estimate perimeter
	Determine perimeter
	Calculate the perimeter of rectangles from measured dimensions
	Describe the change in perimeter when one attribute (length, width) of a rectangle is altered
	Understand the meaning of the ratio of the circumference of a circle to its diameter
	Estimate area
	Determine area
	Represent relationships between areas of rectangles, triangles, and parallelograms using models
	Understand and know how to use the area formula of a triangle
	Understand and know how to use the area formula for a parallelogram
	Understand and apply the formula for the area of a trapezoid
	Use formulas for the areas of rectangles and triangles to find the area of complex shapes
	Derive and use the formula for the area of a triangle and of a parallelogram by comparing it with the formula for the area of a rectangle
	Describe the change in area when one attribute (length, width) of a rectangle is altered
	Determine the surface area of selected solids
	Determine start, elapsed, and end time
	Estimate volumes
	Determine volumes
	Build solids with unit cubes and determine their volumes
	Know the units of measure of volume in both customary and metric units
	Making change up to $100.00
Algebra, Patterns, or Functions	Identify, describe, extend, and create numeric patterns from shapes, tables and graphs
	Analyze and generalize number patterns and state a rule for relationships
	Identify, describe, extend, and create functions from shapes, tables and graphs
	Describe a rule used in a simple grade-level appropriate function
Expressions, Equations, and Inequalities	Use a variable to represent an unknown number
	Evaluate algebraic expressions with one unknown, one operation and whole numbers

		Write simple algebraic expressions in one or two variables
		Use the distributive property in numerical equations and expressions
		Write a number sentence for a problem expressed in words
		Find the unknown in an equation using one operation
		Analyzing functional relationships to explain how a change in one quantity results in a change in another
		Describe patterns of change: constant rate, and increasing or decreasing rate
		Distinguishing between linear and nonlinear functions through informal investigations
		Use technology to graph
	Coordinate Geometry	Identify components of the Cartesian plane, including the *x*-axis, *y*-axis, origin, and quadrants
		Makes and uses coordinate systems to specify locations/objects and to describe paths
		Identify and graph ordered pairs in the four quadrants of the coordinate plane
		Create a graph in a coordinate plane
		Find ordered pairs (positive numbers only) that fit a linear equation, graph the ordered pairs, and draw the line they determine
GEOMETRY		
		Draw points, lines, line segments, rays, and angles with appropriate labels
Geometric Figures and Their Properties		Analyze the properties of plane geometric figures
		Compare or classify quadrilaterals by length of sides and measures of angles
		Compare triangles by sides
		Recognize regular polygons
		Draw 2-dimensional figures by applying significant properties of each
		Identify the diameter, radius, and circumference of a circle
		Sketch prisms, pyramids, cones, and cylinders
		Identify the properties of 2- and 3-dimensional geometric figures using appropriate terminology and vocabulary
		Identify and classify pyramids and prisms by the base
		Analyze the relationship between plane geometric figures and surfaces of solid geometric figures
		Find unknown angles using the properties of triangles, including right, isosceles, and equilateral triangles; parallelograms, including rectangles and rhombuses; and trapezoids

		Measure angles with a protractor, and classify them as acute, right, obtuse, or straight
		Classify triangles by angle measure
		Identify and name angles on a straight line and vertical angles
		Find unknown angles in problems involving angles on a straight line, angles surrounding a point, and vertical angles
		Know that angles on a straight line add up to 180° and angles surrounding a point add up to 360°; justify informally by "surrounding" a point with angles
		Understand why the sum of the interior angles of a triangle is 180° and the sum of the interior angles of a quadrilateral is 360°, and use these properties to solve problems
		Measure, identify, and draw angles, perpendicular and parallel lines, rectangles, triangles, and circles by using appropriate tools
		Recognize that all pairs of vertical angles are congruent
		Apply the Pythagorean theorem
	Congruence, Similarity, Symmetry	Identify the lines of symmetry in a 2-dimensional shape
		Identify or describe geometric figures as similar
		Identify congruent triangles and justify your decisions by referring to sides and angles
		Color maps so that no common edges share the same color
	Transformations	Analyze translations, reflections, and rotations of geometric figures
		Associate an angle with a certain amount of turning; know that angles are measured in degrees
		Predict the results of a flip (reflection), turn (rotation), or slide (translation)
		Identify shapes that have reflectional and rotational symmetry
		Use computer software to explore rotations and reflections of two- and three-dimensional objects
Data Analysis/Statistics		
		Differentiate between categorical and numerical data
		Collect data using measurements, surveys, or experiments and represent the data with tables and graphs with labeling
		Represent data graphically
		Explain which types of displays are appropriate for various sets of data
		Construct, read and interpret tables, charts and graphs (including stem-and-leaf, histogram, bar graph, pie graph, box and whiskers, line graph, scatter plots)
		Determine whether or not a given graph matches a given data set

	Formulate reasonable predictions from a given set of data
	Compare two sets of data related to the same investigation
	Use various measures associated with data to draw conclusions and identify trends
	Find the mean, median, mode, and range of a set of data and describe what each does and does not tell about the data set
	Analyze data collected from a survey or experiment to distinguish between what the data show and what might account for the results
	Uses compute (including spreadsheets) to construct graphs
Probability	
	Understand that probability has value between 0 and 1 inclusive; unlikely events have probability 0, certain events have probability 1, likely events have a higher probability than less likely ones
	Determine possible outcomes of independent events
	Predict and explain the probability of all possible outcomes in an experiment using ratios or fractions
	Make predictions from the results of student-generated experiments using objects
	Make predictions based on experimental and theoretical probabilities
	Conduct experiments or simulations, with and without technology, to model situations and construct sample spaces
	Compare the outcome of an experiment to predictions made about the experiment
	Compare the results of two repetitions of the same grade-level appropriate probability experiment
	Determine the probability of one simple event comprised of equally likely outcomes
	Interpret experimental and theoretical probabilities to determine whether outcomes are equally likely or biased
	Interpret experimental results and theoretical expectations to determine which outcome is most likely to occur if the experiment was conducted again
	Determine the number of possible combinations of given items and displays them in an organized way
	List permutations and combinations of up to five items
Mathematical Connections	Solve applied problems about the volumes of rectangular prisms using multiplication and division and using the appropriate units.

	Solve problems involving perimeters and areas of rectangles, triangles, parallelograms, and trapezoids, using appropriate units.
	Compare temperatures in Celsius and Fahrenheit, knowing that the freezing point of water is 0°C and 32°F and that the boiling point is 100°C and 212°F.
	Identifying negative temperatures (below 0°) on a thermometer
	Add and subtract with money in decimal notation.
	Solving word problems involving elapsed time
	Use variables in contextual situations.
	Use information taken from a graph or equation to answer questions about a problem situation.
	Model simple probabilities by displaying the outcomes for real-world and mathematical problems.
Problem Solving	
	Select and apply appropriate strategies to solve problems
	Solve word problems using calculators/technology as learning tools
	Determine whether information given in a problem-solving situation is sufficient, insufficient, or extraneous
	Given a real-world problem, use an appropriate method (mental arithmetic, estimation, paper-and-pencil, calculator) to correctly solve the problem
Reasoning	Draw logical conclusions about mathematical situations
	Construct "if-then" statements
	Identify simple arguments

Appendix IV: Example of the Adapted Template

Grade 4 Strand	
Number/Number Sense	
	Use place value to read and write whole numbers up to X
	Identify place value form Xth place to Y thousands
	Read and write numbers from Xth place to Y thousands
	Order and compare whole numbers
	Recognize equivalent forms of whole numbers
	Write whole numbers as fractions
	Recognize common fractions as parts of whole (halves, thirds, fourths)
	Compare and order fractions with like denominators
	Compare and order fractions with unlike denominators
	Describe equivalent fractions
	Model and compare rational numbers (fractions and mixed numbers)
	Read, write, and order decimals to Xths
	Represent decimals in different ways
	Express decimals in expanded form
	Order selected fractions, decimals, and whole numbers on a number line
	Compares decimal numbers to Roman numerals
Number Theory	Determine factors, multiples
	Identify square numbers
	Determine factors of numbers up to X
	Apply divisibility rules for 2, 5, 10
	Identify numbers as primes or composites
Number operation/Computation	Know all addition facts to X
	Know all subtraction facts to X
	Know all multiplication facts to X
	Add and subtract to X in different ways
	Multiply 100s by a single digit
	Multiply X digit numbers by Y digit numbers
	Divide X digit number by Y digit numbers
	Recognize that division by 0 is not possible

		Use standard algorithms for addition, subtraction, multiplication, and division
		Construct and analyze algorithms for all operations on whole numbers
		Evaluate algorithms in computation
		Explain the meaning of remainder
		Add and subtract fractions with like and unlike denominators
		Add and subtract with decimals
		Multiply fractions by whole numbers
		Develop and explain strategies for mental computation
		Know and use order of operations
		Use the zero-property of multiplication
		Know that division is not commutative
		Use commutative, associative, and identity properties of addition and multiplication
	Estimation	*Round whole numbers to the nearest Xth place*
		Round decimals to the nearest Xth place
		Use estimation strategies to determine reasonableness of results
		Make and explain adjustments when estimates are used
		Estimate a product or quotient beyond basic facts
Measurement		
	Measurement Tools/Scales	*Use U.S. and metric units to estimate and measure*
		Identify equivalent measurements between units
		Estimate volume of object
		Know that measurements are approximations
		Demonstrate relationships in measures
		Convert within a system
		Use a protractor to measure angles
	Perimeter, Area, and Volume	*Determine perimeter of rectangles and squares*
		Use models to develop formulas for areas
		Determine area of rectangles and squares
		Determine area using rectangle formula
		Describe situations where area is a needed measure
		Compare areas of different shapes
		Find the area of an irregular shape

	Develop formulas to determine surface area
	Explain whether precision or estimate is appropriate for a given measure
	Estimate distance to place or objects
	Use money, compare values, make combinations up to $X
	Use time in problem-solving situations
	Use elapsed time to nearest minute
Algebra, Patterns, or Functions	
	Extend, create patterns of numbers, shapes, or objects
	Analyze a pattern with words, tables, graphs
	Use the rule for a pattern
	Demonstrate understanding of patterns, relations, and functions
	Identify and describe a function rule
	Represent and analyze mathematical situations and structures using algebraic symbols
	Recognize and use commutatitvity of addition
	Recognize inverse relationship of multiplication and division
	Use variables to represent numbers, quantities, or objects
	Solve simple equations or inequalities
	Recognizes differences in linear and nonlinear patterns
	Demonstrate that an equation is a number sentence with two equal quantities
	Construct tables of values with a given function
	Describe how change in one variable affects another related variable
	Describe mathematical relationships using constant rate of change
Expressions, Equations, and Inequalities	*Work with simple linear patterns*
	Use simple equations and inequalities
	Understand the concept of mathematical inequality
	Write a situation requiring an inequality
	Evaluate algebraic expressions
	Use parentheses in solving simple problems
	Use and interpret formulas
	Identify relationships that vary inversely

Coordinate Geometry	*Plot points on a one-quadrant grid*
	Give directions on a coordinate grid
	Describe spatial relationships using coordinate geometry
GEOMETRY	
Geometric Figures and Their Properties	*Draw and label different types of angles, line, or parts of lines*
	Know characteristics of lines
	Identify plane figures and components
	Identify parallel and perpendicular lines
	Compare quadrilaterals
	Classify triangles by lengths of sides and sizes of angles
	Subdivide shapes to obtain different shapes
	Make and test conjectures about geometric properties
	Classify and describe 2- and 3-dimensional objects
	Use attributes to describe 3-dimensional figures
	Identifies components of 3-dimensional figures
	Build a 2-dimensional representation of a prism
	Test conjectures about geometric properties
Congruence, Similarity, Symmetry	*Draw a figure with one line of symmetry*
	Compare attributes of congruent figures
	Solve problems involving congruence
	Identify congruent and noncongruent shapes
	Demonstrates an understanding of similarity
	Identify congruent quadrilaterals
	Makes simple scale drawings
	Color maps with the fewest number of colors
Transformations	*Understand images from flips*
	Simulate translations and reflections using objects
	Identify and draw single translations or flips
	Use transformations to verify that 2 figures are congruent
	Create tessellations using modeling and technology
	Use transformations to verify that 2 figures are similar
	Create rotational designs
	Uses transformations to determine symmetry

Data Analysis/Statistics	
	Describes whether a sample can identify a population
	Collect, organize, and compare data in graphs, Venn diagrams, tables, charts
	Explain sample bias and sample size
	Read data from line plots and pictographs
	Use computers and spreadsheets to organize and display data
	Construct bar graphs, line plots, pictographs, circle graphs
	Describe a trend from a line plot
	Describe characteristics of a set of data
	Describe data using range, mode, and median
	Determine mean, median, and mode for a set of data
	Make predictions based on data
	Understand and reason about use and misuse of statistics
	Communicate conclusions about set of data
	Uses a calculator to determine mean and range
Probability	
	Predict, perform, and record results of probability experiments
	Determine if events are more, less, or equally likely; impossible, or certain
	List all possible outcomes using a tree diagram
	Uses counting techniques for combinations and permutations
	Construct tree diagrams for multistage events
	Determine the theoretical probability of a simple experiment
Mathematical Connections	
	Connect math learning to other subjects, personal experiences, current events
	Use mathematical models to represent and understand quantitative relationships
	Analyze change in various contexts
	Identify mathematics in an everyday situation
	Use simple coordinate systems to find locations on maps

	Use geometric models in different areas of mathematics
	Identify situations where quantities change proportionally
Problem Solving	
	Identify missing information
	Solve real-world problems
	Solve real-world problems where some information is not given
	Use a variety of strategies to solve a problem
	Decide how to break a problem into simpler parts
	Solve nonroutine problems
	Appropriately use a 4-function to solve problems
Reasoning	
	Explain reasonableness of results
	Apply logical reasoning to real-world problems
	Solve problems with simple deductive reasoning
Communication	
	Use appropriate vocabulary
	Communicate and use mathematical language correctly
Grade 5	
Strand	
Number	
Number Sense	*Read, write, or represent decimals using symbols, words, or models*
	Identify irrational numbers and locate them relative to other numbers
	Read, write, or represent fractions or mixed numbers using symbols, models, and words
	Identify or determine equivalent forms of proper fractions
	Explain different interpretations of fractions: as parts of a whole, parts of a set, and divisions of whole numbers by whole numbers
	Understand the relative magnitude of ones, tenths, and hundredths and the relationship of each place value to the place to its right
	Identify numbers less than zero by extending the number line

	Reads, writes, and identifies common percents
	Understand percentages as parts out of 100, use percent notation, and express a part of a whole as a percentage.
	Interpret percents as a part of a hundred. Find decimal and percent equivalents for common fractions and explain why they represent the same value
	Compare, order, round, and expand whole numbers through millions and decimals to thousandths
	Compare or order fractions with or without using the symbols (<, >, or =)
	Compare 2 whole numbers, fractions, and decimals
	Compare, order, or describe decimals with or without using the symbols (<, >, or =)
	Compare and order positive and negative integers
	Identify on a number line the relative position of simple positive fractions, positive mixed numbers, and positive decimals
	Change mixed numbers to improper fractions
	Determine the equivalency between and among fractions, decimals, and percents in contextual situations
	Express ratios in several ways given applied situations recognize and find equivalent ratios
	Reduce fractions to lowest terms
Number Theory	
	Recognize that 1 is neither prime nor composite
	Identify or describe numbers as prime or composite
	Identify and use rules of divisibility for 2, 3, 4, 5, 6, 9, 10
	Identify the greatest common factor
	Identify a common multiple and the least common multiple
	Find the prime factorization of numbers between 1 and 50, express in exponential notation, and understand that every whole number can be expressed as a product of primes
Number Operation/Computation	*Demonstrate computational fluency with addition, subtraction, multiplication, and division of whole numbers*
	Multiply 2-digit numbers by 2-digit numbers

		Divide 3-digit numbers by a single digit
		Add and subtract fractions (including mixed numbers) with different denominators
		Add and subtract fractions with like denominators
		Use models to show an understanding of multiplication and division of fractions
		Multiply and divide fractions to solve problems
		Use mental arithmetic to add or subtract simple decimals
		Add and subtract decimals and verify the reasonableness of the results
		Demonstrate the distributive property of multiplication over addition
		Identify such properties as commutativity, associativity, and distributivity and use them to compute with whole numbers
	Estimation	*Use estimation to verify the reasonableness of a calculation*
		Round to estimate quantities
		Determine from real-world problems whether an estimated or exact answer is acceptable
Measurement		
	Measurement Tools/Scales	*Read customary and metric measurement scales*
		Measure in customary and metric units
		Estimate and determine weight
		Estimate and determine capacity
		Select and use appropriate tools and units
		Draw 2-dimensional figures to specifications using the appropriate tools
		Measure angles
		Convert measurement units to equivalent units within a given system (U.S. customary and metric)
		Differentiate between, and use appropriate units of measures for, two- and three-dimensional objects (i.e., find the perimeter, area, volume)
	Perimeter, Area, and Volume	*Estimate perimeter*
		Determine perimeter
		Calculate the perimeter of rectangles from measured dimensions
		Describe the change in perimeter when one attribute (length, width) of a rectangle is altered

105

	Understand the meaning of the ratio of the circumference of a circle to its diameter
	Estimate area
	Determine area
	Represent relationships between areas of rectangles, triangles, and parallelograms using models
	Understand and know how to use the area formula of a triangle
	Understand and know how to use the area formula for a parallelogram
	Understand and apply the formula for the area of a trapezoid
	Use formulas for the areas of rectangles and triangles to find the area of complex shapes
	Derive and use the formula for the area of a triangle and of a parallelogram by comparing it with the formula for the area of a rectangle
	Describe the change in area when one attribute (length, width) of a rectangle is altered
	Determine the surface area of selected solids
	Determine start, elapsed, and end time
	Estimate volumes
	Determine volumes
	Build solids with unit cubes and determine their volumes
	Know the units of measure of volume in both customary and metric units
	Making change up to $100.00
Algebra, Patterns, or Functions	*Identify, describe, extend, and create numeric patterns from shapes, tables, and graphs*
	Analyze and generalize number patterns and state a rule for relationships
	Identify, describe, extend, and create functions from shapes, tables, and graphs
	Describe a rule used in a simple grade-level appropriate function
Expressions, Equations, and Inequalities	*Use a variable to represent an unknown number*
	Evaluate algebraic expressions with 1 unknown, 1 operation, and whole numbers
	Write simple algebraic expressions in one1 or two variables

		Use the distributive property in numerical equations and expressions
		Write a number sentence for a problem expressed in words
		Find the unknown in an equation using 1 operation
		Analyzing functional relationships to explain how a change in 1 quantity results in a change in another
		Describe patterns of change: Constant rate, and increasing or decreasing rate
		Distinguishing between linear and nonlinear functions through informal investigations
		Use technology to graph
	Coordinate Geometry	*Identify components of the Cartesian plane, including the x-axis, y-axis, origin, and quadrants*
		Makes and uses coordinate systems to specify locations/objects and to describe paths
		Identify and graph ordered pairs in the 4 quadrants of the coordinate plane
		Create a graph in a coordinate plane
		Find ordered pairs (positive numbers only) that fit a linear equation, graph the ordered pairs, and draw the line they determine
GEOMETRY		
		Draw points, lines, line segments, rays, and angles with appropriate labels
	Geometric Figures and Their Properties	*Analyze the properties of plane geometric figures*
		Compare or classify quadrilaterals by length of sides and measures of angles
		Compare triangles by sides
		Recognize regular polygons
		Draw 2-dimensional figures by applying significant properties of each
		Identify the diameter, radius, and circumference of a circle
		Sketch prisms, pyramids, cones, and cylinders
		Identify the properties of 2- and 3-dimensional geometric figures using appropriate terminology and vocabulary.
		Identify and classify pyramids and prisms by the base
		Analyze the relationship between plane geometric figures and surfaces of solid geometric figures

		Find unknown angles using the properties of triangles, including right, isosceles, and equilateral triangles; parallelograms, including rectangles and rhombuses; and trapezoids
		Measure angles with a protractor, and classify them as acute, right, obtuse, or straight
		Classify triangles by angle measure
		Identify and name angles on a straight line and vertical angles
		Find unknown angles in problems involving angles on a straight line, angles surrounding a point, and vertical angles
		Know that angles on a straight line add up to 180° and angles surrounding a point add up to 360°; justify informally by "surrounding" a point with angles
		Understand why the sum of the interior angles of a triangle is 180° and the sum of the interior angles of a quadrilateral is 360°, and use these properties to solve problems
		Measure, identify, and draw angles, perpendicular and parallel lines, rectangles, triangles, and circles by using appropriate tools
		Recognize that all pairs of vertical angles are congruent
		Apply the Pythagorean theorem
	Congruence, Similarity, Symmetry	*Identify the lines of symmetry in a 2-dimensional shape.*
		Identify or describe geometric figures as similar
		Identify congruent triangles and justify your decisions by referring to sides and angles
		Color maps so that no common edges share the same color
	Transformations	*Analyze translations, reflections, and rotations of geometric figures*
		Associate an angle with a certain amount of turning; know that angles are measured in degrees
		Predict the results of a flip (reflection), turn (rotation), or slide (translation)
		Identify shapes that have reflectional and rotational symmetry
		Use computer software to explore rotations and reflections of two- and three-dimensional objects
Data Analysis/Statistics		

	Differentiate between categorical and numerical data
	Collect data using measurements, surveys, or experiments and represent the data with tables and graphs with labeling
	Represent data graphically
	Explain which types of displays are appropriate for various sets of data
	Construct, read, and interpret tables, charts, and graphs (including stem-and-leaf, histogram, bar graph, pie graph, box and whiskers, line graph, scatter plots)
	Determine whether or not a given graph matches a given data set
	Formulate reasonable predictions from a given set of data
	Compare two sets of data related to the same investigation
	Use various measures associated with data to draw conclusions and identify trends
	Find the mean, median, mode, and range of a set of data and describe what each does and does not tell about the data set
	Analyze data collected from a survey or experiment to distinguish between what the data show and what might account for the results
	Uses compute (including spreadsheets) to construct graphs
Probability	
	Understand that probability has value between 0 and 1 inclusive: unlikely events have probability 0; certain events have probability 1; likely events have a higher probability than less likely ones
	Determine possible outcomes of independent events
	Predict and explain the probability of all possible outcomes in an experiment using ratios or fractions
	Make predictions from the results of student-generated experiments using objects
	Make predictions based on experimental and theoretical probabilities
	Conduct experiments or simulations, with and without technology, to model situations and construct sample spaces

	Compare the outcome of an experiment to predictions made about the experiment
	Compare the results of 2 repetitions of the same grade-level appropriate probability experiment
	Determine the probability of 1 simple event comprised of equally likely outcomes
	Interpret experimental and theoretical probabilities to determine whether outcomes are equally likely or biased
	Interpret experimental results and theoretical expectations to determine which outcome is most likely to occur if the experiment was conducted again
	Determine the number of possible combinations of given items and displays them in an organized way
	List permutations and combinations of up to 5 items
Mathematical Connections	*Solve applied problems about the volumes of rectangular prisms using multiplication and division and using the appropriate units*
	Solve problems involving perimeters and areas of rectangles, triangles, parallelograms, and trapezoids, using appropriate units
	Compare temperatures in Celsius and Fahrenheit, knowing that the freezing point of water is 0°C and 32°F and that the boiling point is 100°C and 212°F
	Identifying negative temperatures (below 0°) on a thermometer
	Add and subtract with money in decimal notation
	Solving word problems involving elapsed time
	Use variables in contextual situations
	Use information taken from a graph or equation to answer questions about a problem situation
	Model simple probabilities by displaying the outcomes for real-world and mathematical problems
Problem Solving	
	Select and apply appropriate strategies to solve problems
	Solve word problems using calculators/technology as learning tools

		Determine whether information given in a problem-solving situation is sufficient, insufficient, or extraneous
		Given a real-world problem, use an appropriate method (mental arithmetic, estimation, paper-and-pencil, calculator) to correctly solve the problem
Reasoning		*Draw logical conclusions about mathematical situations*
		Construct "if-then" statements
		Identify simple arguments
Grade 6		
Strand		
Number		
	Number Sense	Identify place value from X to Y
		Use exponential powers
		Evaluate powers of 10 up to 10^6
		Understand and use integers
		Use integers to describe real-world phenomena
		Understand and apply the concept of negative number
		Use and understand decimals
		Write decimals in expanded form
		Order terminating and nonterminating decimals
		Use scientific notation
		Use calculator notation
		Understand fractions as ratios
		Use different forms to symbolize ratios and rates
		Locate numbers (whole, fractions, integers, decimals) on a number line
		Compare and order positive and negative fractions, decimals, and mixed numbers
		Determine equivalency among fractions, decimals, mixed numbers, and percents
		Convert among
		Fractions and decimals
		Fractions and percents
		Decimals and percents
		Use percent to represent a part of a whole
		Model percents greater than 100
		Simplify fractions to lowest terms

		Use proportions to solve problems
		Determine if two ratios form a proportion
	Number Theory	Identify primes and composite numbers
		Express a number in its prime factorization
		Use greatest common factor (divisor)
		Use least common multiple
		Use prime factorizations
		Know divisibility rules for X
	Number Operation/Computation	Recalls facts efficiently
		Multiply X-digit whole numbers by Y-digit whole numbers
		Formulate algorithms using basic operations on
		fractions
		decimals
		Understand relations among basic operations
		Demonstrate that division by 0 is impossible
		Use least common multiple to add and subtract fractions
		Compute with positive and negative numbers
		Uses order of operations
		Describe and illustrate commutative, associative, inverse, and identity properties for addition and multiplication
		Apply the distributive property
		Interpret absolute value of a number as distance from 0
		Divide fractions
		Divide mixed numbers
		Find percent of number
		Understand meaning of square roots
	Estimation	Round numbers using a variety of techniques
		Estimate results of computations
		Estimate the reasonableness of results
		Estimate the reasonableness of results using a calculator
		Understand the concept of significant figures and round answers appropriately
		Estimate with fractions and decimals
Measurement		Estimate angle measure

Measurement Tools/Scales	Determine distance between two points on a scale drawing
	Measure to the nearest X unit
	Convert units of length, weight, capacity within a system
	Calculate elapsed time
	Create a new figure by increasing or decreasing original measures
	Compare objects according to measures
	Estimates measure of object and then measures
	Selects appropriate unit of measure
	Knows where an exact answer is needed
Perimeter, Area, and Volume	Estimate perimeter measure perimeter of figures
	Develop formulas for perimeter an area of specified figures
	Find the circumference of a circle
	Estimate area
	Estimate and measure area of triangles and quadrilaterals
	Use formulas to determine perimeter
	Use formulas to determine areas
	Find the surface area of 3-dimensional figures
	Find the volume of selected 3-dimensional figures
	prisms
	cylinders
	Convert between Celsius and Fahrenheit
Algebra, Patterns, or Functions	Solve problems using numeric and geometric patterns
	Continue a pattern
	Find missing terms in a pattern
	Determine a verbal rule for a function given input and output
	Express rules with and without variables
	Communicate a recursive pattern
	Create functions tables and graphs
	Use variables in contexts
	Translate between words and symbols
Expressions, Equations, and Inequalities	Write and solve 1-step inequalities
	Solve an equation for an unknown; linear equation; 1 unknown

		Explain how change in one variable relates to another variable
		Uses properties of equality
		Simplify expressions using order of operations
		Uses associative, commutative, and distributive properties to work with expressions
		Simplify expressions by combining like terms
		Evaluate an expression by substitution
		Understand direct proportion
		Understand inverse proportion
		Use proportional reasoning to solve problems
	Coordinate Geometry	Plot coordinates
		Identify coordinates in Cartesian plane
		Compare parallel and perpendicular lines
		Use graphing calculators to develop the concept of slope
		by hand
		by scientific calculator
		Graph discrete functions
		Graph continuous functions
GEOMETRY		
	Geometric Figures and Their Properties	Identify 2-d and 3-dimensional figures based on attributes and properties
		Classify quadrilaterals based on attributes
		Classify triangles by angles
		Classify angles by measure
		Identify and use parts of a circle
		Identify complementary and supplementary angles
		Identify spheres, cones, cylinders, prisms, and pyramids
		Identify concave and convex polygons
		Create nets for 3-dimensional figures
		Draw 2-dimensional views of 3-dimensional figures
		Know that sum of measures of angles of a triangle is 180 degrees
		Know that the sum of the measures of the angles about a point is 360 degrees
		Solve problems with angle measures
		Understand the concept of pi

	Produce constructions with compass and straightedge
	Apply geometric formulas to solve problems
	Develop formulas for perimeter, area, and volumes
	Solve surface area problems
Congruence, Similarity, Symmetry	Identify and use congruent, similar, or symmetrical geometric figures
	Draw a figure using lines of symmetry
	Recognize and draw congruent and similar figures
Transformations	Identify line symmetries
	Identify rotational symmetries
	Find the results of transformations on a figure
	Draw the results of transformations
	Creates tessellations
	Work with shapes on a coordinate grid with transformations
Data Analysis/Statistics	
	Interpret information from bar graphs, line graphs, and circle graphs
	Design an investigation, collect, organize, and display data
	Formulate questions from contextual data
	Construct histogram, line graph, scatter plot, stem-and-leaf plot, double bar graphs, tally charts, frequency tables, circle graphs, line graphs, box-and-whisker plots
	Identify ways of selecting a sample
	Explain whether a sample reflects a population
	Identify data with sampling errors and explain any bias
	Identify a trend from displayed data
	Find and use mean, median, mode, range
	Understand how inclusion or exclusion of outliers affects measures of central tendency
	Evaluate truth of a statement based on data
	Demonstrate the meaning of random sample
	Use technology to create graphs
	Use computer technology to manipulate data
Probability	

	Find the probability of a simple event
	Express probabilities as ratios, percents, and decimals
	Analyze whether a game is fair or unfair
	Name all possible outcomes from an experiment
	Solve problems involving combinations
	Determine all possible arrangements of items in a list
	Determine all possible outcomes for compound events
	Understand the multiplication property for probabilities
	Compare the results of 2 repetitions of the same experiment
	Find odds for or against something
	Determine the theoretical probability of a given event
	Use the fundamental counting principle
	Identify and describe complementary events
Discrete Mathematics	
	Find the shortest route on a map
Problem Solving	
	Solve problems with decimals, percents, fractions, and proportions
	Solve real-world problems involving elapsed time and in different time zones
	Solve problems with percent of increase or percent of decrease
	Apply strategies to solve problems
	Solve nonroutine word problems
	Solve multistep consumer problems
	Solves problems in real-world contexts
Reasoning	
	Use informal deductive reasoning
	Formulate and justify mathematical conjectures
	Agrees/disagrees with a given argument about geometric relationships and gives supporting evidence or counterexample

	Make and test conjectures
	Agree with or refute mathematical arguments
Communication	
	Represent problems mathematically and with ethnology
	Use appropriate mathematical language and symbols

Appendix V: Standards with Less Agreement

Kindergarten Standards with Less Agreement

The set of kindergarten standards for which less than 25 percent of the 37 states agreed follows:

Number

Count by 2s, 5s, 10s (9) 24%

Represent equivalent forms of same number with materials (_+_=_+_) (9) 24%

Part-whole relationships (8) 22%

Identify halves (7) 19%

Count on (7) 19%

Model halves, thirds, fourths (6) 16%

Locate numbers on number line (5) 14%

Describe use of numerals in real life (2) 5%

Operations

Add and subtract numbers (8) 22%

Create stories for addition and subtraction (5) 14%

Use symbols: +, -, = (5) 14%

Identify and evaluate reasonableness of answers (3) 8%

Demonstrate addition and subtraction with technology (2) 5%

Relationship between addition and subtraction (2) 5%

Use repeated addition to model multiplication (1) 3%

Measurement

Identify calendar and clock as tools to measure time (9) 24%

Read time to hour (unspecified or both digital/analog) (9) 24%

Estimate measurement of objects (8) 22%

Identify and use tools to measure objects (8) 22%

Measure with standard units (4) 11%

Use money (3) 8%

Identify time of everyday events (3) 8%

Determine value of small set of coins (2) 5%

Geometry

Describe 3-dimensional objects (9) 24%

Describe similarities and differences of 2- and 3-dimensional shapes (9) 24%

Investigate symmetry of 2-dimensional shapes (6) 16%

Use flips, slides, and turns (6) 16%

Explore congruence (4) 11%

Use technology to create shapes (3) 8%

Probability and Data Analysis

Describe events as likely/unlikely, possible/impossible, fair/unfair (9) 24%

Pose questions for the purpose of collecting data (9) 24%

Make predictions from data (4) 11%

Describe results of simple experiments (3) 8%

Use mode and range concepts to describe data (3) 8%

Algebra (including Patterns and Functions)

Translate patterns from one form to another (e.g., symbols to shapes) (4) 11%

Explore notions of change (4) 11%

Use technology to explore patterns (2) 5%
Working with missing addends (oral or written) (2) 5%
Use symbols to represent missing/unknown quantities in patterns (2) 5%

Problem Solving and Mathematical Processes

Select operation to solve story problems (3) 8%
Solve story problems presented orally using + or - (3) 8%
Make precise calculations and check results (3) 8%
Use patterns to solve problems (1) 3%

Reasoning

Explain how a problem was solved (6) 16%
Build simple arguments and justify results (3) 8%

Connections

Relate everyday language to mathematical language/symbols (8) 22%
Represent mathematical ideas (7) 19%
Apply mathematics in other content areas (3) 8%
Connect ideas within mathematics (2) 5%

Grade 1 Standards with Less Agreement

The set of Grade 1 standards for which less than 25 percent of the 38 states agreed follows.

Number

        Model fractional parts of a set (1/2, 1/4) (9) 24%

        Demonstrate 1-to-1 correspondence among sets of objects (8) 21%

        Represent a number up to 10 in different ways (6) 16%

        Know differences in odds and evens (6) 16%

        Determine the value of a digit based on its position in a number (6) 16%

        Use ordinal numbers (3) 8%

        Identify any ordinal number (3) 8%

        Identify numbers as odd or even (3) 8%

        Show correct sequence of cardinal numbers to 50 (2) 5%

        Use of 0 (2) 5%

        Group and regroup objects into 1s, 10s, and 100s (2) 5%

        Use zero as a placeholder (1) 3%

        Count by 1s, 2s, 5s, 10s, 100s (1) 3%

Number Operations

        Create stories involving addition (6) 16%

        Use a calculator (appropriately) (5) 13%

        Know relationship between addition and subtraction (5) 13%

        Use strategies to estimate sums (5) 13%

        Add and subtract without regrouping (4) 11%

        Use repeated addition to find the sum when given the number of groups (3 or fewer) and given the same number of concrete objects in each group (5 or fewer) (3) 8%

        Add and subtract in horizontal and vertical form (3) 8%

        Memorize facts (3) 8%

        Memorize facts for addition (3) 8%

        Memorize facts for subtraction (3) 8%

        Solve problems involving addition and subtraction with 2-digit numbers using manipulatives (3) 8%

        Division by sharing (2) 5%

        Use strategies to estimate sums—rounding (2) 5%

        Use repeated subtraction when given the total number of concrete objects in each group to find the number of groups (1) 3%

        Add numbers through 100 (1) 3%

        Subtract numbers through 100 (1) 3%

        Verify that subtraction is not commutative (1) 3%

        Add fractions with like denominators (halves and fourths) (1) 3%

        Use strategies to estimate sums—compatible numbers (1) 3%

Measurement

        Read calendar with days, weeks, months, year (9) 24%

        Order events in time (9) 24%

        Use calendar/yesterday, today, tomorrow, etc. (8) 21%

        Measure to the nearest inch or centimeter (8) 21%

        Name days of week and seasons of year and months (7) 18%

Make combinations and name total value of coins (7) 18%
Use calendar (6) 16%
Select appropriate unit (4) 11%
Estimate using nonstandard units (4) 11%
Know uniform units are needed to measure (4) 11%
Tell time to half hour (nearest X minutes) (4) 11%
Calculate elapsed time (4) 11%
Know some simple conversions, hours in day, months in year, etc. (4) 11%
Use comparative words to compare attributes (3) 8%
Estimate number of objects (3) 8%
Identify measurable attributes (3) 8%
Compare estimate to actual measurement (3) 8%
Use vocabulary to describe length of events (1) 3%
Demonstrate conceptual knowledge of perimeter (1) 3%
Demonstrate conceptual knowledge of area (1) 3%
Measure capacity with standard units in cups (1) 3%
Use benchmarks for estimating (1) 3%
Estimate and measure perimeter in standard and nonstandard units (1) 3%
Estimate and count the number of units to determine area (1) 3%
Tell time to half hour (nearest X minutes)—analog clocks (1) 3%
Tell time to half hour (nearest X minutes)—digital clocks (1) 3%
Convert among units in the same system (1) 3%
Count money through $1 (1) 3%

Geometry

Describe objects with characteristics (9) 24%
Identify congruent shapes (9) 24%
Describe 3-dimensional objects in terms of 2-dimensional shapes asrepresented in real life
    (6) 16%
Combine shapes to form new shape (6) 16%
Identify 3-dimensional objects (5) 13%
Give and follow directions about location (5) 13%
Draw a shape with given characteristics (4) 11%
Name, classify, and describe 2-dimensional objects (4) 11%
Compare and contrast plane and solid geometric shapes (4) 11%
Combine shapes to fill in area (3) 8%
Compare relative position (3) 8%
Identify shapes by attributes (2) 5%
Describe spatial relationships using coordinate geometry (2) 5%
Recognize 3-dimensional figures (2) 5%
Identify a congruent shape that has been rotated and/or reflected (2) 5%
    circle, square, triangle, rectangle (1) 3%
Identify objects based on descriptions (1) 3%
Investigate the symmetry of 2-dimensional shapes (1) 3%
Color pictures with the least number of colors (1) 3%
Identify lines of symmetry (1) 3%
Identify and draw similar shapes (1) 3%

Describe location with directional maps (1) 3%

Probability

Describe events as likely or unlikely (2) 5%

Making predictions (2) 5%

Conduct simple experiments with more than 2 outcomes and predict results (2) 5%

Describe the result of dropping a coin (1) 3%

Report probability experiment results using spinners (1) 3%

Recognize if spinners are fair or unfair (1) 3%

Make arrangements to represent a number of combinations (1) 3%

Data Analysis

Use physical objects to build graphs (8) 21%

Create questions about data (8) 21%

Obtain information from a display (graph) (8) 21%

Answer questions about a pictograph (5) 13%

Extract information from different sources (5) 13%

Make predictions based on data (5) 13%

Make a true statement based on the simple concepts of mode and range (3) 8%

Organize data (2) 5%

Formulate questions from data (2) 5%

Use technology for data gathering (2) 5%

Understand the organization of graphs, labels, etc. (1) 3%

Collect, organize, and report data using Venn diagrams (1) 3%

Algebra

Classify and sort objects; use Venn diagrams (6) 16%

Growing patterns (6) 16%

Use a variable in contextual situations (6) 16%

Identify and extend patterns (5) 13%

Recognize x-element pattern units (5) 13%

Describe a rule for a pattern (5) 13%

Find a missing element of a pattern (5) 13%

Identify patterns in real-world situations (4) 11%

Extend simple patterns (3) 8%

Continue a pattern given a rule (3) 8%

Use input/output model for a function (3) 8%

Concept of function (2) 5%

Recognize and extend linear pattern (2) 5%

Demonstrate equivalency of two numerical expressions written as a number sentence (2) 5%

Associative property (1) 3%

Solve an equation with an unknown (1) 3%

Describe how change in one variable affects another (1) 3%

Problem Solving

Solve story problems that require one- or two-step solutions using multiple strategies (8) 21%

Solve story problems using concrete objects and pictures (6) 16%

Select appropriate strategy to solve problems (6) 16%

Given a problem, write a number sentence (6) 16%

Use a problem-solving model, with guidance, that incorporates understanding the problem, making a plan, carrying out the plan, and evaluating the solution for reasonableness (4) 11%

Solve problems using visualization, spatial reasoning, and geometric modeling (4) 11%

Defining problems (2) 5%

Given a number sentence, write a problem (2) 5%

Predict solution to problem in a given situation with numbers (1) 3%

Make precise calculations and check validity of results in problem contexts (1) 3%

Reasoning

Explain the reasoning used and justify the procedures selected in solving a problem (7) 18%

Justifying results (4) 11%

Build simple arguments (1) 3%

Make a conclusion based on evidence (1) 3%

Justify reasonableness of results (1) 3%

Connections

Create math models (6) 16%

Model real-life situations involving addition (6) 16%

Use correct operation to solve a real-world problem (3) 8%

Relate everyday language to mathematical language and symbols (2) 5%

Mathematics across the content (1) 3%

Identify inequality in a "real" situation (1) 3%

Grade 2 Standards with Less Agreement

The set of Grade 2 standards for which less than 25 percent of the 36 states agreed follows:

Number

    Represent numbers, read, write, order, compare to 100 (6) 17%

    Determine relative magnitude (sense of site, benchmarks) (5) 14%

    Identify 10 more or less/100 more or less (5) 14%

    Recognize equivalent forms of common fractions (2) 6%

    Represent numbers, read, write, order, compare to 200 (1) 3%

Number Operations

    Add and subtract two whole numbers with 3 digits (8) 22%

    Methods/tools for computation paper and pencil/algorithms (8) 22%

    Add three or more 1- or 2-digit numbers (7) 19%

    Methods/tools for computation technology/calculators (7) 19%

    Using CGI strategies (e.g., part/part/wholes comparison) (6) 17%

    Use strategies to estimate sums/quantities—rounding (6) 17%

    Understand the effect of addition and subtraction on numbers (5) 14%

    Add and subtract decimals using money (5) 14%

    Fluency with basic facts—multiplication facts to 5×5 (5) 14%

    Know how to use horizontal and vertical notation for addition and subtraction (4) 11%

    Methods/tools for computation—invented algorithms (4) 11%

    Methods/tools for computation—compose/decompose (4) 11%

    Equivalent representations on sums/differences (3) 8%

    Verify that subtraction is not commutative (1) 3%

    Use strategies to estimate sums/quantities—compatible numbers (1) 3%

    Methods/tools for computation number line (1) 3%

Measurement

    Use benchmarks for estimating (8) 22%

    Use calendar to solve problems (e.g., finding dates) (8) 22%

    Compare and order measurement results (8) 22%

    Tell time nearest 30 minutes (8) 22%

    Calculate elapsed time (7) 19%

    Tell time nearest 1 hour (7) 19%

    Recognize that different units of measure (Standard/nonstandard) will result in different number results (6) 17%

    Identify measurable attributes (4) 11%

    Order events in time (3) 8%

    Linear measurement nearest half-inch (3) 8%

    Money nearest $5 (3) 8%

    Linear measurement nearest foot (2) 6%

    Money nearest $2 (2) 6%

    Linear measurement nearest precision (1) 3%

    Money nearest $10 (1) 3%

Geometry

    Draw a shape with given characteristics (8) 22%

    Identify transformations—reflections/flips/mirror images (8) 22%

Use spatial visualization (8) 22%
Identify shapes by attributes (2d) (7) 19%
Identify and draw similar shapes (7) 19%
Compare shapes using attributes (3-dimensional) (7) 19%
Identify transformations—rotations/turns (7) 19%
Compare and contrast 2- and 3-dimensional shapes (6) 17%
Identify transformations—translations/slides (6) 17%
Locate points on a line (5) 14%
Construct/build 3-dimensional figures (2) 6%
Determine parallel, perpendicular lines (1) 3%

Probability

Make arrangements to represent a number of combinations (5) 14%
Compare the results of experiments (4) 11%
Compare results to predictions (3) 8%
Use models/manipulatives (3) 8%
Use graphs, such as organizational lists and tree diagrams (3) 8%
Recognize fairness with fair/unfair spinners (2) 6%

Data Analysis

Collect data systematically using surveys (8) 22%
Organize and display data using Venn diagrams (7) 19%
Organize and display data using line plots/line graphs (4) 11%
Identify features of data sets (range, mode, and/or median) (4) 11%
Use technology for data gathering, displaying, or analyzing (3) 8%
Collect data systematically using tally marks (3) 8%
Recognize/represent data sets in more than one way (3) 8%

Algebra

Use a variable in contextual situations and noncontextual (8) 22%
Connect math symbols and language (7) 19%
Use model for a function (e.g., input/output, T-chart) (7) 19%
Sort, classify, and order objects by attributes (7) 19%
Translate among representations of patterns (6) 17%
Demonstrate understanding of inequality (6) 17%
Find a missing element of a pattern (5) 14%
Identify patterns in real world (5) 14%
Express mathematical relationships (in one and two variables; expressions; number
    sentence) (2) 6%
Describe how change in one variable affects another (1) 3%

Grade 3 Standards with Less Agreement

The set of Grade 3 standards for which less than 25 percent of the 42 states agreed follows:

Number Sense

Locate fractions on a number line (10) 24%

Compose and decompose whole numbers (9) 21%

Use proper fractions in context (9) 21%

Determine equivalency among decimals, fractions, and percents as related to money (9) 21%

Rounding numbers to place value (9) 21%

Compare 2 decimals through tenths and hundredths (8) 19%

Make models for fractions (8) 19%

Determines factors of numbers up to 100 with chart (4) 10%

Mixed numbers (4) 10%

Order 3 or more decimals through tenths and hundredths (3) 7%

Read and write Roman numerals to X (3) 7%

Know difference in natural and whole numbers (2) 5%

Equivalent fractions (2) 5%

Computation

Compute division problems with no remainder (8) 19%

Use alternative algorithms for computation (6) 14%

Understand the meaning of remainder in division (6) 14%

Teach problem solving strategies using word problems (5) 12%

Invent algorithms to solve problems (4) 10%

Model division as partitioning (3) 7%

Understand the effect of multiplying by 10 and 100 (3) 7%

Recognize the use of the distributive property (2) 5%

Algebra

Use a variable in a contextual situation (10) 24%

Write an equation or expression for a situation (10) 24%

Analyze/describe change in a variable (10) 24%

Explain equality (8) 19%

Determine equal expressions (8) 19%

Use properties of whole numbers—associative (7) 17%

Use properties of whole numbers—identity (6) 14%

Create a word problem to match a given number sentence (4) 10%

Recognize multiplication and division as inverse operations (3) 7%

Compare two patterns (1) 2%

Measurement

Create referents to standard units (9) 21%

Describe different units of measurement for length and weight and how organized (8) 19%

Understand differences between standard and nonstandard units of measure (7) 17%

Compare and order by measure (7) 17%

Use a variety of measuring devices including the 3 mentioned formulas for perimeter and area (4) 10%

Geometry/Spatial Sense

 Compare similarities and differences in similar and congruent figures (10) 24%

 Classify angles (9) 21%

 Recognize similar shapes (8) 19%

 Locate numbers on number line (4) 10%

 Draw net of 3 dimensions (4) 10%

 Identify simple tessellations (3) 7%

 Recognize the same shape in different positions (2) 5%

Data Analysis/Statistics

 Scales greater than 1 (7) 17%

 Determine range of a data set (6) 14%

 Explain how graphs can support different points of view (6) 14%

 Recognize elements in the union and intersections of Venn diagrams (6) 14%

 Make charts and tables—circle graphs (5) 12%

 Determine the median for a data set (5) 12%

 Represent data in more than one way (5) 12%

 Determine the mean with concrete objects (3) 7%

 Recognize data as categorical or numerical (3) 7%

 Use a computer to create bar and circle graphs (2) 5%

 Use a calculator to compare data (2) 5%

 Use mode to solve a problem (1) 2%

Probability

 Compare experiment result to predict (9) 21%

 Combinations (9) 21%

 Graph outcomes of probability experiments and predict (8) 19%

 Compare the results of two repetitions of the same experiment (5) 12%

 Analyze the fairness of different spinners (experimental) (4) 10%

 Analyze the results of rolling a die (1) 2%

Grade 4 Standards with Less Agreement

The set of Grade 4 standards for which less than 25 percent of the 41 states agreed follows:

Number/Number Sense
> Express decimals in expanded form (10) 24%
> Identify numbers as primes or composites (6) 15%
> Identify square numbers (4) 10%
> Apply divisibility rules for 2, 5, 10 (4) 10%
> Compare decimal numbers to Roman numerals (1) 2%

Number Operation/Computation
> Explain the meaning of remainder (10) 24%
> Compute with money (9) 22%
> Multiply a single digit by multiples of 10, 100, 1,000 (7) 17%
> Use order of operations (7) 17%
> Round decimals to the nearest Xth place (range from whole number places to .001) (7) 17%
> Multiply and divide fractions and whole numbers (2) 5%

Measurement
> Find areas of irregular shapes (10) 24%
> Explain whether precision or estimate is appropriate (8) 20%
> Know measurements are approximations (3) 7%

Algebra, Patterns, or Functions
> Plot points on coordinate grid to demonstrate transformations (*see also* Geometry) (7) 17%

Data Analysis/Statistics
> Describe a trend for a line plot (9) 22%
> Differentiate appropriate uses and misuses of data (8) 20%
> Describe whether a sample can describe a population (7) 17%

Mathematical Connections
> Connect math learning to other subjects, personal experiences, current events (7) 17%
> Use relationships in math concepts to learn other math concepts (6) 15%

Problem Solving
> Evaluate the appropriateness of a solution (9) 22%
> Identify missing information as relevant/nonrelevant (6) 15%
> Build new mathematical knowledge (6) 15%
> Identify appropriate use of technology to solve problems (4) 10%
> Solve nonroutine problems (3) 7%

Reasoning
> Explain reasonableness of results (10) 24%
> Apply logical reasoning to real-world problems (5) 12%
> Solve problems with simple deductive reasoning (5) 12%
> Investigate mathematical arguments (5) 12%
> Make or test generalizations/assumptions (4) 10%
> Know when it is appropriate to estimate (2) 5%

Communication
> Communicate and use mathematical language correctly (8) 20%
> Communicate math thinking coherently (8) 20%

Grade 5 Standards with Less Agreement

The set of Grade 5 standards for which less than 25 percent of the 41 states agreed follows:

Number

    Interpret percents as a part of 100 (9) 22%

    Express ratios in several ways given applied situations; recognize and find equivalent ratios (9) 22%

    Identify the greatest common factor (8) 20%

    Find the prime factorization of numbers between 1 and 50, express in exponential notation, and understand that every whole number can be expressed as a product of primes (8) 20%

    Change mixed numbers to improper fractions (6) 15%

    Reduce fractions to lowest terms (6) 15%

    Explain different interpretations of fractions: as parts of a whole, parts of a set, and divisions of whole numbers by whole numbers (5) 12%

    Compare and order positive and negative integers (5) 12%

    Recognize equivalent forms of whole numbers (4) 10%

    Use exponential powers (4) 10%

    Identify place value form Xth place to Y thousands (3) 7%

    Determine factors, multiples (3) 7%

    Identify square numbers (3) 7%

    Use integers to describe real-world phenomena (3) 7%

    Determine factors of numbers up to X (2) 5%

    Identify irrational numbers and locate them relative to other numbers (2) 5%

    Use place value to read and write whole numbers up to X (1) 2%

    Read and write numbers from Xth place to Y thousands (1) 2%

    Describe equivalent fractions (1) 2%

    Evaluate powers of 10 up to 10^6 (1) 2%

    Understand and apply the concept of negative number (1) 2%

    Understand fractions as ratios (1) 2%

Number Operations

    Solve problems using operations with whole numbers (10) 24%

    Demonstrate the distributive property of multiplication over addition (9) 22%

    Solve world problems that involve decimals, [common] fractions, and money (8) 20%

    Use order of operations (8) 20%

    Model multiplication/division of whole numbers and decimal fractions (7) 17%

    Describe and illustrate commutative, associative, inverse, and identity properties for addition and multiplication (7) 17%

    Multiply and divide fractions to solve problems (6) 15%

    Use mental arithmetic with addition, subtraction, multiplication, and/or division to solve problems (5) 12%

    Select, sequence, and use appropriate operations to solve multistep, whole number problems (4) 10%

    Understand relations among basic operations (3) 7%

    Demonstrate that division by 0 is impossible (3) 7%

    Recall facts efficiently (2) 5%

Formulate algorithms using basic operations on fractions and decimals (2) 5%

Divide fractions (1) 2%

Measurement

Estimate or read temperatures (10) 24%

Understand and know how to use the area formula of a triangle (9) 22%

Estimate perimeter (8) 20%

Understand and know how to use the area formula for a parallelogram (8) 20%

Know the units of measure of volume in both customary and metric units (8) 20%

Estimate and determine capacity (7) 17%

Calculate the perimeter of rectangles from measured dimensions (7) 17%

Determine the surface area of selected solids (7) 17%

Determine degree of accuracy (precision) (7) 17%

Read customary and metric measurement scales (6) 15%

Describe the change in perimeter when one attribute (length, width) of a rectangle is altered (6) 15%

Estimate angles using benchmark angles (5) 12%

Differentiate between, and use appropriate units of measures for, 2- and 3-dimensional objects (i.e., find the perimeter, area, volume) (4) 10%

Understand the meaning of the ratio of the circumference of a circle to its diameter (4) 10%

Use formulas for the areas of rectangles and triangles to find the area of complex shapes (4) 10%

Build solids with unit cubes and determine their volumes (4) 10%

Draw two-dimensional figures to specifications using the appropriate tools (3) 7%

Understand and apply the formula for the area of a trapezoid (3) 7%

Describe the change in area when one attribute (length, width) of a rectangle is altered (3) 7%

Represent relationships between areas of rectangles, triangles, and parallelograms using models (2) 5%

Derive and use the formula for the area of a triangle and of a parallelogram by comparing it with the formula for the area of a rectangle (2) 5%

Making change up to $100 (2) 5%

Geometry

Identify or describe geometric figures as similar (10) 24%

Analyze translations, reflections, and rotations of geometric figures (10) 24%

Draw points, lines, line segments, rays, and angles with appropriate labels (9) 22%

Compare or classify quadrilaterals by length of sides and measures of angles (9) 22%

Recognize regular polygons (9) 22%

Identify the diameter, radius, and circumference of a circle (9) 22%

Measure, identify, and draw angles, perpendicular and parallel lines, rectangles, triangles, and circles by using appropriate tools (9) 22%

Identify the lines of symmetry in a 2-dimensional shape (9) 22%

Measure angles with a protractor, and classify them as acute, right, obtuse, or straight (7) 17%

Understand why the sum of the interior angles of a triangle is 180°, the sum of the interior angles of a quadrilateral is 360°, and use these properties to solve problems (7) 17%

Predict or create 3-dimensional figures from nets (6) 15%

Subdivide shapes to obtain different shapes (4) 10%

Draw 2-dimensional figures by applying significant properties of each (4) 10%

Create tessellations (4) 10%

Draw and label different types of angles, line, or parts of lines (3) 7%

Sketch prisms, pyramids, cones, and cylinders (3) 7%

Analyze the relationship between plane geometric figures and surfaces of solid geometric figures (3) 7%

Know that angles on a straight line add up to 180° and angles surrounding a point add up to 360°; justify informally by "surrounding" a point with angles (3) 7%

Identify and classify pyramids and prisms by the base (2) 5%

Find unknown angles using the properties of triangles, including right, isosceles, and equilateral triangles; parallelograms, including rectangles and rhombuses; and trapezoids (2) 5%

Associate an angle with a certain amount of turning; know that angles are measured in degrees (2) 5%

Draw 2-dimensional views of 3-dimensional figures (2) 5%

Classify and describe 2- and 3-dimensional objects (1) 2%

Test conjectures about geometric properties (1) 2%

Identify and name angles on a straight line and vertical angles (1) 2%

Find unknown angles in problems involving angles on a straight line, angles surrounding a point, and vertical angles (1) 2%

Recognize that all pairs of vertical angles are congruent (1) 2%

Identify spheres, cones, cylinders, prisms, and pyramids (1) 2%

Probability

Conduct experiments or simulations, with and without technology, to model situations and construct sample spaces (9) 22%

Determine possible outcomes of independent events (8) 20%

Make predictions based on experimental or theoretical probabilities (8) 20%

Make predictions from the results of student-generated experiments using objects (7) 17%

Determine the number of possible combinations of given items and displays them in an organized way (7) 17%

Compare the outcome of an experiment to predictions made about the experiment (5) 12%

Interpret experimental results and theoretical expectations to determine which outcome is most likely to occur if the experiment was conducted again (2) 5%

Find the probability of a simple event (2) 5%

Compare the results of two repetitions of the same grade-level appropriate probability experiment (1) 2%

Determine the probability of 1 simple event comprised of equally likely outcomes (1) 2%

Interpret experimental and theoretical probabilities to determine whether outcomes are equally likely or biased (1) 2%

List permutations and combinations of up to 5 items (1) 2%

Determine the theoretical probability of a given event (1) 2%

Data Analysis

Design an investigation; collect, organize, and display data (10) 24%

Use various measures associated with data to draw conclusions and identify trends (8) 20%

Compare 2 sets of data related to the same investigation (7) 17%

Describe effects of data collection methods (6) 15%

Analyze data collected from a survey or experiment to distinguish between what the data show and what might account for the results (5) 12%

Formulate questions from contextual data (4) 10%

Evaluate truth of a statement based on data (4) 10%

Differentiate between categorical and numerical data (3) 7%

Uses compute (including spreadsheets) to construct graphs (2) 5%

Identify a trend from displayed data (2) 5%

Represent data graphically (1) 2%

Determine whether or not a given graph matches a given data set (1) 2%

Algebra

Write a number sentence for a problem expressed in words (9) 22%

Describe patterns of change: constant rate and increasing or decreasing rate (9) 22%

Use the distributive property in numerical equations and expressions (7) 17%

Analyze functional relationships to explain how a change in one quantity results in a change in another (7) 17%

Identify and graph ordered pairs in the 4 quadrants of the coordinate plane (7) 17%

Use patterns to solve problems (7) 17%

Write and solve 1-step inequalities (2) 5%

Use associative, commutative, and distributive properties to work with expressions (2) 5%

Use variables to represent numbers, quantities, or objects (1) 2%

Distinguish between linear and nonlinear functions through informal investigations (1) 2%

Identify components of the Cartesian plane, including the x-axis, y-axis, origin, and quadrants (1) 2%

Find ordered pairs (positive numbers only) that fit a linear equation, graph the ordered pairs, and draw the line they determine (1) 2%

Determine a verbal rule for a function given input and output (1) 2%

Grade 6 Standards with Less Agreement

The set of Grade 6 standards for which less than 25 percent of the 41 states agreed follows:

Number

Use proportions to solve problems (9) 22%

Write decimals in expanded form (8) 20%

Know divisibility rules for X (8) 20%

Identify place value from X to Y (6) 15%

Model percents greater than 100 (6) 15%

Use scientific notation (3) 7%

Evaluate powers of 10 up to 10^6 (1) 2%

Number Operations

Multiply X digit whole numbers by Y digit whole numbers (8) 20%

Apply the distributive property (8) 20%

Estimate the reasonableness of results using a calculator (6) 15%

Understand the concept of significant figures and round answers appropriately (4) 10%

Recalls facts efficiently (3) 7%

Understand meaning of square roots (3) 7%

Demonstrate that division by 0 is impossible (1) 2%

Interpret absolute value of a number as distance from 0 (1) 2%

Measurement

Find the surface area of 3-dimensional figures (9) 22%

Calculate elapsed time (6) 15%

Convert units between systems (6) 15%

Geometry

Identify complementary and supplementary angles (10) 24%

Know that sum of measures of angles of a triangle is 180 degrees (10) 24%

Understand the concept of pi (9) 22%

Recognize and draw congruent and similar figures (8) 20%

Work with shapes on a coordinate grid with transformations (6) 15%

Create nets for 3-dimensional figures (5) 12%

Draw a figure using lines of symmetry (4) 10%

Create tessellations (4) 10%

Identify concave and convex polygons (3) 7%

Produce constructions with compass and straightedge (3) 7%

Probability

Solve problems involving combinations (7) 17%

Analyze whether a game is fair or unfair (6) 15%

Determine all possible outcomes for compound events (6) 15%

Determine all possible arrangements of items in a list (3) 7%

Find odds for or against something (3) 7%

Compare the results of two repetitions of the same experiment (1) 2%

Use the fundamental counting principle (1) 2%

Identify and describe complementary events (1) 2%

Data Analysis

Identify ways of selecting a sample (9) 22%

Evaluate truth of a statement based on data (7) 17%

Explain whether a sample reflects a population (6) 15%

Understand how inclusion or exclusion of outliers affects measures of central tendency (6) 15%

Identify a trend from displayed data (5) 12%

Identify data with sampling errors and explain any bias (3) 7%

Demonstrate the meaning of random sample (2) 5%

Algebra

Use associative, commutative, and distributive properties to work with expressions (10) 24%

Solve problems using numeric and geometric patterns (8) 20%

Write and solve 1-step inequalities (8) 20%

Use graphing calculators to develop the concept of slope (7) 17%

Use proportional reasoning to solve problems (5) 12%

Find missing terms in a pattern (4) 10%

Communicate a recursive pattern (4) 10%

Compare parallel and perpendicular lines (4) 10%

Simplify expressions by combining like terms (2) 5%

Use properties of equality (1) 2%

Understand direct proportion (1) 2%

Understand inverse proportion (1) 2%

Grade 7 Standards with Less Agreement

The set of Grade 7 standards for which less than 25 percent of the 42 states agreed follows:

Number

    Writes percents greater than 100% and less than 1% (9) 21%

    All forms and percents (8) 19%

    Decimals (repeating and terminating) and fractions (7) 17%

    Identify pi and square roots of nonperfect squares as irrational numbers (7) 17%

    Model place value of decimals (5) 12%

    Differentiate between rational and irrational numbers (5) 12%

    Expanded form and standard form (2) 5%

    Understand derived quantities (2) 5%

    Know that every rational number is a repeating or terminating decimal and vice versa (1) 2%

Number Operations

    Justify why estimation would be used rather than an exact approximation (10) 24%

    Convert rates from one unit to another (9) 21%

    Use a variety of rounding techniques (8) 19%

    Calculate rates of change (7) 17%

    Determine equivalent ratios (6) 14%

    Analyze algorithms (5) 12%

    Identify when an approximation is appropriate (5) 12%

    Develop algorithms for integer operations (4) 10%

    Calculate percents of increase and decrease (4) 10%

    Use mental arithmetic to compute with simple fractions, decimals, and powers (4) 10%

    Use calculators to compute with decimal numbers with precision from the Xth place (4) 10%

Measurement

    Determine area of composite shapes (10) 24%

    Estimate accurately to the Xth of a unit (9) 21%

    Explain how changing one dimension has an effect on area and volume measure (8) 19%

    Distinguish between and uses precision and accuracy (5) 12%

    Understand the difference on surface area and volume (4) 10%

    Describe relationships among linear dimensions (1) 2%

    Justify standard formulas for areas of selected figures (1) 2%

Geometry

    Recognize geometric relationships among 2-dimensional and 3-dimensional figures (10) 24%

    Determine missing angles (8) 19%

    Apply the Pythagorean theorem (8) 19%

    Construct scale drawings (8) 19%

    Graph similar figures using a dilation (7) 17%

    Determine sufficient properties that define a specific 2-dimensional object (6) 14%

    Construct nets for 3-dimensional figures (6) 14%

    Use a scale factor to solve problems (6) 14%

    Draw figures given components (5) 12%

Understand the value of pi from geometric and numeric settings (5) 12%
Perspective drawing (5) 12%
Recognize the relation between central angles and intersected arcs (4) 10%
Use geometric properties to reason about figures/real-life objects (4) 10%
Understand conditions for congruency in triangles (4) 10%
Apply congruence or similarity properties to find missing parts of figures (4) 10%
Know that a scale drawing is an example of similarity (4) 10%
Construct tessellations (3) 7%
Determine symmetry found in a transformation (2) 5%
Understand properties preserved under different transformations (2) 5%
Show that two triangles are similar using AAA or SAS or SSS (1) 2%

Probability

Identify sample space (10) 24%
Represent outcomes as a list, chart, picture, or tree diagram (10) 24%
Determine the probability of a compound event (8) 19%
Determine all possible outcomes involving combinations and permutations (7) 17%
Fundamental counting principal (6) 14%
Compare the results of the repetitions of the same experiment (4) 10%
Analyze games of chance to determine fairness (3) 7%
Know that the probability of independent events is the product of the probabilities (2) 5%
Compute mathematical odds (2) 5%
Explain when events are mutually exclusive (2) 5%
Explore the concept of randomness (1) 2%

Data Analysis

Use computer applications to manipulate data (8) 19%
Quartiles (7) 17%
Determine the appropriate measure of central tendency to use (7) 17%
Recognize misuses of data (7) 17%
Interquartile range (6) 14%
Describe how adding data changes measures of central tendency (6) 14%
Identify a sample relevant to a question and population (5) 12%
Collect, organize, display data in line plots (4) 10%
Venn diagrams (4) 10%
Use spreadsheets to work with data (3) 7%
Maximum and minimum (2) 5%
Present collected data to support an opinion (2) 5%

Algebra

Describe how change in one variable affects a related variable (10) 24%
Express quantitative relationships by using algebraic terminology, expressions, equations, inequalities, and graphs (10) 24%
Create representations of linear patterns (10) 24%
Graph data points (10) 24%
Generalize relations (9) 21%
Apply properties of rational number operations and justify process: Commutative, associative, identity, inverse, distributive (7) 17%
Solve proportions (7) 17%

Explain simplification of expressions and equations using order of operations (7) 17%
Use the distance formula d = rt with real data (7) 17%
Define slope (7) 17%
Use variables in contextual situations (6) 14%
Use correct algebra terminology (6) 14%
Identify equivalent equations (6) 14%
Graph solution sets of inequalities (6) 14%
Graph and interpret linear and nonlinear functions (5) 12%
Find slope from graph (5) 12%
Use a calculator to work with patterns (4) 10%
Use technology to determine a rule for a linear pattern (4) 10%
Solve equations and inequalities over rational numbers (4) 10%
Draw line given slope and 1 point on the line or 2 points on the line (3) 7%
Recognize recursive patterns (2) 5%
Solve equations with technology (2) 5%
Use recursive formulas (1) 2%
Plot transformations on coordinate planes (1) 2%

Grade 8 Standards with Less Agreement

The set of Grade 8 standards for which less than 25 percent of the 39 states agreed follows:

Number

Understand 0 and negative integers as exponents (9) 23%

Explain and illustrate relationships between subsets of real numbers (9) 23%

Determine percent of increase or decrease (9) 23%

Solve problems with simple and compound interest (9) 23%

Use the laws of exponents (7) 18%

Determine unit rates (7) 18%

Approximate square roots (7) 18%

Recognize nonrepeating nonterminating decimals as irrational numbers (6) 15%

Identify equivalent forms of real numbers (6) 15%

Determine when ratios form a proportion (6) 15%

Convert among representations of real numbers (5) 13%

Identify and explain absolute value (5) 13%

Use mental arithmetic to compute with simple fractions, decimals, and powers (4) 10%

Express answers to appropriate place or degree of precision (4) 10%

Identify and convert between equivalent forms of rational numbers (3) 8%

Order and compare numbers rational (3) 8%

Write numbers in expanded form (3) 8%

Add, subtract, multiply, and divide with fluency (3) 8%

Use the distributive property to factor expressions and numbers (3) 8%

Verify calculator results by estimation (3) 8%

Identify pi and square roots of nonperfect squares as irrational numbers (2) 5%

Find square roots (2) 5%

Explain advantages and disadvantages of the use of percents, decimals, and ratios (2) 5%

Demonstrate an understanding of rational numbers: fractions, decimals, percents, integers (1) 3%

Identify and use primes and composites (1) 3%

Use mental computation, calculators, technology, and written and verbal communication with real numbers (1) 3%

Determine square of an integer (1) 3%

Determine square root of an integer (1) 3%

Identify and justify whether properties (closure, identity, inverse, commutative, and associative) for sets of numbers (1) 3%

Estimate the solutions for problem situations involving square and cube roots (1) 3%

Measurement

Know how perimeter, area, and volume are affected by change of scale (6) 15%

Recognize and use precision of measurement (6) 15%

Sum of interior and exterior angles of polygons (3) 8%

Convert units of length, weight, or capacity from metric to customary and vice versa (2) 5%

Justify standard formulas for areas of selected figures (1) 3%

Geometry

Sketch figures from characteristics (9) 23%

Construct geometric figures in 2-dimension (9) 23%

Create tessellations (9) 23%

Build models from different views (and draw) (8) 21%

Find uses of geometric concepts in the nature of real world (8) 21%

Apply the triangle inequality theorem (7) 18%

Construct congruent or similar figures (7) 18%

Describe the effect of transformations on figures (2- and 3-dimension) (7) 18%

Know angle relationships with different types of lines (parallelism) (6) 15%

Calculate distances in the coordinate plane (5) 13%

Identify tangents and secants, etc. (5) 13%

Special right triangles (4) 10%

Identify parts of congruent figures (3) 8%

Recognize the relationship between arcs and intercepting angles (2) 5%

Explain slope as a representation of rate of change (2) 5%

Identify basic elements of geometric figures (1) 3%

Know the Pythagorean theorem (1) 3%

Graph a line when the slope and a point or when 2 points are known (1) 3%

Define basic trigonometric ratios in right triangles (1) 3%

Apply proportions and right triangles trigonometric ratios to solve problems (1) 3%

Probability

Calculate the probability of complementary events (6) 15%

Calculate the probability of mutually exclusive events (6) 15%

Make predictions from probability (5) 13%

Compare the results of 2 repetitions of the same grade-level experiments (4) 10%

Analyze games of chance to determine if they are fair or unfair (4) 10%

Convert between odds and probabilities (4) 10%

Computer relative frequencies (3) 8%

Determine the probability of a compound event (1) 3%

Determine whether outcomes are likely or unlikely (1) 3%

Use Pascal's triangle to solve problems (1) 3%

Data Analysis

Use information from a variety of displays and analyze the validity of statistical conclusions (9) 23%

Represent data with the most appropriate graph—bar graph (8) 21%

Represent data with the most appropriate graph—stem-and-leaf plots (8) 21%

Represent data with the most appropriate graph—histograms (8) 21%

Represent data with the most appropriate graph—line graph (6) 15%

Determine measures of central tendency—quartiles (4) 10%

Compare data sets from 2 populations (4) 10%

Determine measures of central tendency (3) 8%

Calculate weighted averages (3) 8%

Determine measures of central tendency—interquartile range (2) 5%

Represent data with the most appropriate graph—frequency table (1) 3%

Distinguish between causation and correlation (1) 3%

Discrete versus continuous data (1) 3%

Algebra

Understand and use variables (9) 23%

Simplify monomials and polynomials (8) 21%

Identify slope as a rate of change (8) 21%

Recognize and apply simple formulas (7) 18%

Classify variables as independent or dependent (6) 15%

Determine when a relation is a function (4) 10%

Solve quadratic equations with real roots (4) 10%

Communicate iterative or recursive patterns (3) 8%

Identify the domain and range of functions—quadratic (3) 8%

Solve problems with the distributive property (2) 5%

Write a linear equation given slope and a point (2) 5%

Direct and indirect variation (2) 5%

Identify the domain and range of functions—linear (2) 5%

Identify the domain and range of functions—exponential (2) 5%

Describe how a change in the value of a constant in a linear or quadratic equation affects the related graphs (2) 5%

Solve equations: 1-step (1) 3%

Factor simple quadratics (1) 3%

Determine the midpoint given 2 points on a line (1) 3%

Evaluate polynomial expression to a power for given values of the variable (1) 3%

Identify the domain and range of functions (1) 3%

Use formulas to solve problems involving exponential growth and decay (1) 3%

Grade 9 Standards with Less Agreement

Comparison of Grade 9 Standards

Only 4 states had separate Grade 9 standards that could be used for comparison. A comparison is not possible here so all are listed.

Number and Operations

Demonstrate computational fluency with all rational numbers

Use proportional reasoning to model and solve real-life problems involving direct and inverse variation

Compare, order, and determine equivalent forms for rational and irrational numbers

Evaluate and write numerical expressions involving integer exponents

Apply scientific notation to perform computations, solve problems, and write representations of numbers

Explain the effects of operation on the magnitude of quantities

Estimate the solutions for problem situations involving square and cube roots

Identify and describe differences among the following sets: Natural numbers

Identify and describe differences among the following sets: Whole numbers

Identify and describe differences among the following sets: Integers

Identify and describe differences among the following sets: Rational numbers

Identify and describe differences among the following sets: Irrational numbers

Identify and justify whether properties (closure, identity, inverse, commutative, and associative) hold for sets of numbers

Distinguish between an exact and an approximate answer, and recognize errors

Simplify and perform basic operations on numerical expressions involving radicals

Measurement

Solve problems using indirect measurement

Convert rates within the same measurement system

Use unit analysis to check computations involving measurement

Solve problems involving unit conversion

Distinguish between precision and accuracy

Demonstrate and explain how the scale of a measuring instrument determines the precision of that instrument

Use significant digits in computational problems

Demonstrate and explain how relative measurement error is compounded when determining absolute error

Determine appropriate units and scales to use when solving measurement problems

Use the ratio of lengths in similar 2- or 3-dimensional figures to calculate the ratio of areas or volumes

Use scale drawings and right triangle trigonometry to solve problems

Algebra

Use order of operations to simplify or rewrite variable expressions

Generalize patterns using functions or relationships

Model real-life situations using linear expressions, equations, and inequalities

Use equivalent forms of equations and inequalities to solve real-life problems

Translate among tabular, graphical, and algebraic representations of functions and real-life situations

Interpret and solve systems of linear equations using graphing, substitution, elimination, and matrices using technology

Determine if a relation is a function and use appropriate notation

Identify and describe the characteristics of families of linear functions, with and without technology

Compare linear functions algebraically in terms of their rates of change and intercepts

Explain how the graph of a linear function changes as the coefficients or constants are changed

Describe and compare characteristics of the following families of functions: Exponential

Write and use equivalent forms of equations and inequalities in problem situations

Solve and interpret the meaning of 2-by-2 systems of linear equations graphically, by substitution, and by elimination, with and without technology

Identify independent and dependent variables in real-life relationships

Evaluate polynomial expression for given values of the variable

Translate between the characteristics defining a line, its equation, and graph

Graph and interpret linear inequalities in one or two variables and systems of linear inequalities

Identify the domain and range of functions

Analyze real-life relationships that can be modeled by linear functions

Demonstrate the relationship among 0s of a function, roots of equations, and solutions of equations

Describe and compare characteristics of the following families of functions: Linear

Describe and compare characteristics of the following families of functions: Quadratic

Use formulas to solve problems involving exponential growth and decay

Find linear equations that represent lines that pass through a given set of ordered pairs

Solve quadratic equations with real roots

Perform computation with polynomials

Simplify rational expressions

Describe how a change in the value of a constant in a linear or quadratic equation affects the related graphs

Geometry

Use coordinate methods to solve and interpret problems

Perform translations and line reflections on the coordinate plane

Explain slope as a representation of rate of change

Graph a line when the slope and a point or when two points are known

Define basic trigonometric ratios in right triangles

Apply proportions and right triangles trigonometric ratios to solve problems

Analyze 2-dimensional figures in a coordinate plane

Data Analysis

Create a scatter plot for a set of bivariate data, sketch the line of best fit, and interpret the slope of the line of best fit

Determine the most appropriate measure of central tendency for a set of data based on its distribution

Identify trends in data and support conclusions by using distribution characteristics such as patterns, clusters, and outliers

Analyze and interpret frequency distributions based on spread, symmetry, skewness, clusters, and outliers

Describe and compare various types of studies and identify possible misuses of statistical data

Create a scatter plot form a set of data and determine if the relationship is linear or nonlinear

Classify data as univariate or bivariate and as quantitative or qualitative

Describe characteristics and limitations of sampling methods and analyze the effects of random versus biased sampling

Make inferences about relationships in bivariant data, and recognize the difference between evidence of relationship and causation

Probability

Define probability in terms of sample spaces, outcomes, and events

Compute probabilities using geometric models and basic counting techniques, such as combinations and permutations

Use counting techniques and the fundamental counting principle to determine the total number of possible outcomes for situations

Use simulations to estimate probabilities

Explain the relationship between the probability of an event occurring and the odds of an event occurring and compute one given the other

Follow and interpret processes expressed in flow charts

Integrated Mathematics I Standards with Less Agreement

Comparison of Integrated Mathematics I Course Standards

Only 3 states allowed for comparison of Integrated Mathematics I as a separate course. Standards appearing in at least 1 of the 3 states are indicated below.

Number and Operations
Use laws of exponents
Compare real numbers
Simplify square roots
Use the associative, commutative, identity, inverse, and distributive properties
Compute with real numbers (1) 33%
Use integral exponents on integers and algebraic expressions

Measurement
Use dimensional analysis to organize conversions and computations
Apply formulas to find measures
Choose and apply appropriate units and tools to measure

Algebra
Compute with polynomials
Represent problem situations symbolically using algebraic expressions, sequences, tree
    diagrams, geometric figures, and graphs
Solve linear equations
Find solutions sets of linear inequalities
Interpret a graph representing a given situation
Find the domain and range of a function
Model real-world problems with systems of equations and inequalities
Simplify and compare expression
Sketch a reasonable graph for a given relationship
Understand the concept of a function
Find the slope, x-intercept, and y-intercept of a line
Write the equation of a line in point-slope form
Write the equation of a line that models a data set
Use a graph to estimate the solution of a pair of linear equations
Understand and use the substitution method
Use elimination to solve a system of equations
Graph quadratic, cubic, exponential, and radical equations
Solve quadratic equations using the quadratic formula

Geometry
Find the perimeters and areas of polygons
Prove and use the Pythagorean theorem
Identify and describe types of polygons
Apply transformations to polygons to determine congruence and similarity
Use properties of congruent and similar quadrilaterals to solve problems
Describe relationships among the faces, edges, and vertices of polyhedra
Describe symmetries of geometric solids

Data Analysis
Find measures of central tendencies for a set of data

Construct a line plot, a histogram, a stem-and-leaf plot, a frequency table, a scatter plot

Identify clusters, gaps, and outliers for a set of data

Find a linear transformation

Find the mean absolute deviation for a set of data

Find the standard deviation for a set of data

Summarize and interpret sets of data using center and variability

Plot the least square regression line from a set of data

Compare sets of data using scatter plots and the line $y = x$

Recognize patterns in tables and graphs modeled by linear equations

Probability

Use empirical and theoretical probabilities

Design and use simulations to estimate answers in probability

Use the law of large numbers to understand situations involving chance

Understand independent events

Understand the concept of a probability distribution

Determine probabilities using permutations and combinations

Discrete Mathematics

Use a recursion function

Perform row and column sums for matrix equations

Construct vertex-edge graph models

Construct digraphs

Use Euler paths and circuits to solve real-world problems

Develop the skill of algorithmic problem solving

Use recursion to describe a fractal

Use an adjacency matrix to describe a vertex-edge graph

Problem Solving

Use problem-solving strategies

Reasoning

Decide whether a solution is reasonable

Use properties of real numbers to justify steps in solutions

Decide whether an algebraic equation is sometimes, never, or always true

Distinguish between inductive and deductive reasoning

Use counterexamples to show that statements are false

Construct valid arguments

Standards for Algebra I Course with Less Agreement
Comparison of Algebra I Course Standards
The set of algebra I standards for which less than 25 percent of the 16 states agreed follows:
Number and Operations
> Simplify expressions using order of operations (2) 13%
> Use number systems (2) 13%
> Compute with exponential and radical expressions (1) 6%
> Identify the results of an algorithm (1) 6%
> Compare real number expressions (1) 6%

Measurement
> Solve problems algebraically that involve: Surface area of cylinders, prisms (3) 19%
> Determine the appropriateness of measurements in terms of precision, accuracy, and approximate error (2) 13%
> Use sine, cosine, and tangent ratios with and without a calculator (1) 6%
> Complete error analysis for measurement data (1) 6%
> Use dimensional analysis to organize conversions and computations (1) 6%

Algebra
> Represent situations with the following: Quadratic function (3) 19%
> Represent situations with the following: Exponential function (3) 19%
> Simplify sums, differences, products, and quotients of rational expressions (3) 19%
> Factor polynomials using: Greatest common factor (3) 19%
> Factor polynomials using: Difference of squares (3) 19%
> Factor polynomials using: Perfect square trinomials (3) 19%
> Students simplify fractions with polynomials in the numerator and denominator by factoring both and reducing them to lowest terms (3) 19%
> Use a vector or matrix to organize data in a problem (3) 19%
> Add, subtract scalar multiples and multiply matrices (3) 19%
> Recognize the parent graph of functions like $y = k$, $y = x$, $y = |x|$, and predict effects of transformations on parent graph (3) 19%
> Use manipulatives, models, and simulations to represent problems and situations involving patterns (2) 13%
> Solve problems involving sequences with recurrence relations and infinite sequences (2) 13%
> Simplify expressions (2) 13%
> Identify situations modeled by common relations (2) 13%
> Use concepts such as prime, factor, divisor, multiple, and divisibility in algebraic expressions (2) 13%
> Graph the solution of an equation or inequality (2) 13%
> Represent situations with the following: Trigonometric function (1) 6%
> Determines the maximum or minimum points of a graph and estimates the area under a curve (1) 6%
> Use basic types of functions (1) 6%
> Use basic types of functions: Linear (1) 6%
> Use basic types of functions: Exponential (1) 6%
> Use basic types of functions: Periodic (1) 6%
> Use basic types of functions: Power (1) 6%

Use basic types of functions: Rational (1) 6%

Use basic types of functions: Squares (1) 6%

Use basic types of functions: Quadratics (1) 6%

Use basic types of functions: Square roots (1) 6%

Represent situations that involve variable quantities with expressions, equations, inequalities, and matrices (1) 6%

Determine characteristics of a relation including: Relative maximum/minimum values (1) 6%

Determine characteristics of a relation including: Zeroes (1) 6%

Determine characteristics of a relation including: Intercepts, (1) 6%

Recognize that $ax + by + c = 0$ is the equation of a line (1) 6%

Write the solution of an equation in set notation (1) 6%

Understand and use such operations as taking the opposite, finding the reciprocal, taking a root, and raising to a fractional power (1) 6%

Use vector and matrix operations to solve problems (1) 6%

Geometry

Compute area, surface area, and volume (2) 13%

Use the Pythagorean theorem to find values and solve problems (2) 13%

Find the measure of corresponding parts of similar figures (1) 6%

Solve 2- and 3-dimensional problems with coordinates (1) 6%

Use parallelism and perpendicularity to solve problems (1) 6%

Data Analysis

Compare various methods of data reporting, including: Scatter plots, (2) 13%

Compare various methods of data reporting, including: Stem-and-leaf plots (2) 13%

Identify characteristics of a data set, including measurement or categorical and univariate or bivariate (2) 13%

Explain how sample size or transformations of data affect shape, center, and spread (2) 13%

Compare various methods of data reporting, including: Histograms (1) 6%

Compare various methods of data reporting, including: Box-and-whisker plots (1) 6%

Compare various methods of data reporting, including: Line graphs (1) 6%

Summarizes data and makes predictions from a sample (1) 6%

Use sequences and series (1) 6%

Problem Solving

Use estimation strategies (1) 6%

Probability

Estimate probabilities given data in lists or graphs (1) 6%

Use basic laws of probability (1) 6%

Reasoning

Justify steps in simplifying expressions and solving equations (3) 19%

Understand the logic of an equation (2) 13%

Decide whether a statement is always true, sometimes, or never (1) 6%

Distinguish between inductive and deductive reasoning (1) 6%

Identify the hypothesis and conclusion in a deduction (1) 6%

Use counterexamples to support arguments (1) 6%

Connections

Use formulas or equations of functions to calculate outcomes of exponential growth and decay (2) 13%

Use algebraic techniques to make financial and economic decisions (1) 6%

Grade 10 Standards Comparison with Less Agreement

There were 5 states that had standards allowing for a Grade 10 comparison of standards. These are independent of courses. The first group, the set of standards for which at least 2 of the 5 states agreed, follows:

Number and Operations

Judge the reasonableness of numerical computations and their results (4) 80%

Compare subsets of the real number system with regard to their properties (3) 60%

Compare subsets of the real number system with regard to their properties: Commutative (3) 60%

Compare subsets of the real number system with regard to their properties: Associative (3) 60%

Compare subsets of the real number system with regard to their properties: Identity (3) 60%

Compare subsets of the real number system with regard to their properties: Inverse (3) 60%

Compare subsets of the real number system with regard to their properties: Distributive (3) 60%

Apply properties of exponents to simplify expressions or solve equations (3) 60%

Use a variety of representations to demonstrate an understanding of very large and very small numbers (2) 40%

Compare subsets of the real number system with regard to their properties: Closure (2) 40%

Solve problems involving proportions (2) 40%

Measurement

Explain how a small error may lead to a large error in calculated results (2) 40%

Calculate relative error (2) 40%

Explain the difference in absolute error and relative error (2) 40%

Give examples of how the same absolute error can be problematic in one situation but not in others (2) 40%

Algebra

Generalize patterns using explicitly or recursively defined functions (4) 80%

Use and solve systems of linear and quadratic equations or inequalities with two variables (4) 80%

Compare various forms of representations of patterns (3) 60%

Identify quantitative relationships and determine the types of functions that might model the situations (3) 60%

Solve equations for a specific variable (3) 60%

Understand and compare the properties of linear, exponential, and quadratic functions (2) 40%

Geometry

Make, test, and establish the validity of conjectures (4) 80%

Construct geometric figures using dynamic geometry software or not (3) 60%

Solve problems involving parts of the same circle (3) 60%

Use inductive and deductive reasoning to establish the validity of geometric conjectures (3) 60%

Solve volume and surface area problems with 3-dimensional figures (3) 60%

Use and apply constructions to represent translations, reflections, rotations, and dilations (2) 40%

Data Analysis

Select and use an appropriate display to represent and describe a set of data (3) 60%

Formulate questions, design studies and collect data about a characteristic (2) 40%

Display bivariate data where at least one variable is categorical (2) 40%

Identify outliers on a data display and describe how they affect measures of central tendency (2) 40%

Interpret the relationship between two variables using multiple graphical displays and statistical measures (2) 40%

Interpret and analyze data in various display forms (2) 40%

Probability

Use and describe how to compute the probability of a compound event (3) 60%

Model problems dealing with uncertainty with area models (2) 40%

The second group, the set of tenth grade standards listed by only 1 state, follows:

Number and Operations

Use real numbers to solve problems

Apply operation to real numbers using mental computation or paper-and-pencil calculations and technology as needed

Connect physical, verbal, and symbolic representations of irrational numbers

Explain the meaning of nth root

Use factorial notation and computations to represents and solve problems

Approximate the nth root of a given number greater than 0

Apply prime numbers and prime factorization

Measurement

Use unit analysis to solve problems involving rates

Determine the measures of central and inscribed angles and their associated arcs

Algebra

Describe the effects of parameter changes on quadratic and exponential functions

Use symbolic algebra to represent and solve problems that involve quadratic relationships

Use and solve equivalent form of equations and inequalities

Analyze quadratics by investigating rates of change and intercepts

Describe the relationship between slope of a line through the origin and the tangent function of the angle created by the line and the positive x-axis

Geometry

Formally define and explain key aspects of geometric figures

Recognize and explain the necessity for certain terms to remain undefined

Prove the Pythagorean theorem

Apply relationships among surface areas and among volumes of similar solids

Make conjectures and solve problems involving 2-dimensional objects represented with Cartesian coordinates

Draw representations of 3-dimensional geometric objects from different perspectives

Draw or use visual models to solve problems

Data Analysis

> Draw inferences from collections of data
>
> Apply statistical concepts to solve problems
>
> Distinguish between a parameter and a statistic
>
> Given one-variable quantitative data, display the distribution, describe its shape, and calculate summary statistics
>
> Given a scatter plot, determine a type of function that models the data
>
> Describe measures of center and range of data sets
>
> Represent and analyze bivariate data
>
> Provide examples and explain how a statistic may or may not be an attribute of the entire population
>
> Compute frequency, mean, median, mode, and range

Probability

> Differentiate and explain the relationship between the probability of an event the odds of an event and compute one given the other
>
> Use experimental or theoretical probability to solve problems
>
> Solve problems involving dependent and independent events

Geometry Course Standards with Less Agreement

The set of geometry course standards for which less than 25 percent of the 14 states agreed follows:

Algebra

Use coordinate geometry to find the equations of parallel and perpendicular lines (3) 21%

Properties of figures

Classify polyhedra according to their properties (3) 21%

Identify Euclidean solids (2) 14%

Constructions

Construct with precision a circle graph to represent data (1) 7%

Using Geometry

Solve real-life and mathematical problems using properties and theorems related to circles (3) 21%

Use the geometric mean to find missing lengths in right triangles (3) 21%

Trigonometry

Know and use $\sin^2(x) + \cos^2(x) = 1$ (2) 14%

Transformations

Create tessellations (3) 21%

Use matrix operations to describe the transformation of polygons in the coordinate plane (2) 14%

Identify the coordinates of the vertices of the image of a given polygon under a transformation (2) 14%

Analyze sets of data from geometric contexts to determine what, if any, relationships exist (2) 14%

Determine the effect of scale factors on dilations (1) 7%

Reasoning

Use and interpret Venn diagrams (3) 21%

Recognize the limitations of using inductive reasoning (2) 14%

Use of/justify theorems related to Pythagorean theorem (2) 14%

Use valid forms of deductive reasoning, including law of syllogism (2) 14%

Prove and apply theorems involving segments divided proportionally (1) 7%

Write and interpret statements in "if–then" and "if and only if" form (1) 7%

Integrated Mathematics II with Less Agreement

Comparison of Integrated Mathematics II Standards
Only 4 states allowed for the comparison of standards for Integrated Mathematics II as a separate course. All standards given by those states are listed below.

Number and Operations
>Understand and use rational and irrational numbers
>Recognize the order of real numbers
>Compute with real numbers
>Apply the properties of real numbers to different subsets of numbers
>Recognize the hierarch of the complex number system
>Model the structure of complex numbers
>Use rational exponents on real numbers and all operations on complex numbers
>Compare real numbers
>Simplify square roots
>Use the associative, commutative, identity, inverse, and distributive properties

Measurement
>Use trigonometry as a method to measure indirectly
>Understand error in measurement
>Derive formulas to find measure such as length, area, and volume in real-world context
>Use trigonometry as a method to measure indirectly
>Derive and apply formulas relating angle measure and arc degree
>Choose and apply appropriate units and tools to measure quantities

Algebra
>Relate trigonometric relationships to the area of a triangle and to general solutions of triangles
>Solve and model quadratic equalities or inequalities both algebraically and graphically
>Define the trigonometric functions in terms of a unit circle
>Represent problem situations symbolically using algebraic expressions, sequences, tree diagrams, geometric figures, and graphs
>Represent problem situations symbolically
>Develop meaning for the conic sections
>Model real-world problems with systems of equations and inequalities
>Use algebraic relationships to analyze the conic sections
>Use circular functions to study and model periodic real-world phenomena
>Use function vocabulary and notation
>Solve equations with complex roots
>Analyze inverse functions
>Develop an understanding of and use the composition of functions and transformations
>Use transformations on figures and functions in the coordinate plane
>Combine functions using the basic operations and the composition of 2 functions
>Manipulate symbolic representations to explore concepts at an abstract level
>Choose appropriate representations to facilitate the solving of a problem
>Model vector quantities both algebraically and geometrically
>Represent graphically the sum and difference of 2 complex numbers
>Model the composition of transformations

Determine the effects of changing parameters of the graphs of functions

Use polynomial, trigonometric, and exponential functions to model real-world relationships

Use graphing utilities to create and explore geometric and algebraic models

Represent and analyze functions using verbal descriptions, tables, equations, and graphic forms

Analyze the effect of parametric changes on graphs of equations

Apply linear, exponential, and quadratic functions in the solution of problems

Apply and interpret transformations to functions

Model real-world situations with the appropriate function

Apply axiomatic structure to algebra and geometry

Evaluate and form the composition of functions

Develop methods to solve trigonometric equations and verify trigonometric functions

Graph quadratic functions

Simplify and compare expressions

Find solutions sets of linear inequalities

Interpret a graph representing a given situation

Find the domain and range of a function

Find the slope, rate of change, x-intercept, and y-intercept of a line

Use a graph to estimate the solution of a pair of linear equations

Understand and use the substitution method

Geometry

Use basic transformations to demonstrate similarity and congruence of figures

Prove and apply theorems related to length of segments in a circle

Use properties of congruence and similarity to solve problems

Use special right triangles to solve problems

Find the perimeters and areas of polygons

Prove and use the Pythagorean theorem

Identify and differentiate between direct and indirect isometries

Perform the basic geometric constructions

Identify and describe various triangles

Construct tangents to circles and circumscribe and inscribe circles

Identify and describe types of polygons

Apply transformations to polygons to determine congruence and similarity

Use properties of congruent and similar quadrilaterals to solve problems

Use transformation in the coordinate plane

Justify procedures for basic geometric constructions

Determine distance and slope between 2 points in the coordinate plane

Data Analysis

Use statistical methods, including scatter plots and lines of best fit to make predictions

Use curve fitting to fit data

Apply the normal curve and its properties to familiar contexts

Describe association between two variables by interpreting a scatter plot

Interpret correlation coefficients

Understand that a correlation between two variables does not imply causation

Recognize patterns in tables and graphs modeled by linear equations

Design a statistical experiment to study a problem and communicate the outcome,
   including dispersion

Make predictions from the least squares regression line or its equation

Construct a line plot, a histogram, a stem-and-leaf plot, a frequency table, a scatter plot

Find measures of central tendencies for a set of data

Plot the least square regression line from a set of data

Probability

Design and use simulations to estimate answers in probability

Use empirical and theoretical probabilities

Understand independent events

Understand the concept of a probability distribution

Determine probabilities using permutations and combinations

Discrete Mathematics

Use Euler paths and circuits to solve real-world problems

Construct vertex-edge graph models

Develop the skill of algorithmic problem solving

Use an adjacency matrix to describe a vertex-edge graph

Perform row and column sums for matrix equations

Reasoning

Distinguish between inductive and deductive reasoning

Construct valid arguments

Decide whether a solution is reasonable

Use properties of real numbers to justify steps in solutions

Decide whether an algebraic equation is sometimes, never, or always true

Use counterexamples to show that statements are false

Algebra II Standards with Less Agreement

Comparison of Algebra II Course Standards

The set of Algebra II standards for which less than 25 percent of the 14 states agreed follows:

Number and Operations

Order hierarchically sets of numbers (2) 14%

Use properties of exponents (2) 14%

Explains the limitations of calculators and computers in solving problems (2) 14%

Use the field properties with complex numbers (commutative, associative, identity, inverse, and distributive property of multiplication over addition) (1) 7%

Uses vector or matrix operations to solve problems (1) 7%

Use the concept of infinity (1) 7%

Measurement

Express rates of change as a ratio of 2 different measures (1) 7%

Calculate lengths of arcs and sector areas (1) 7%

Complete an error analysis for measurement data (1) 7%

Determine how errors can compound with multiple computations (1) 7%

Determine how imprecision is reasonable (1) 7%

Solve problems using formulas for volumes (1) 7%

Estimate area under a curve (1) 7%

Estimate instantaneous rate of change (1) 7%

Polar coordinates (1) 7%

Algebra

Distinguish between a sequence and a series (3) 21%

Explore families of functions and recognize and graph various functions: Logarithmic (3) 21%

Solve equations containing radicals and exponents (3) 21%

Solve matrix equations using a calculator (3) 21%

Understand the binomial theorem and use it to expand expressions (3) 21%

Solve logarithmic and exponential inequalities and equations (3) 21%

Perform the transformations of stretching, shifting, and reflecting the graphs of different functions (3) 21%

Use amplitude, frequency, phase, and period of trigonometric functions (3) 21%

Use laws of sines and cosines (3) 21%

Use the discriminant to determine the nature of the roots (2) 14%

Define a function (2) 14%

Model problems with a system of no more than 3 equations (2) 14%

Use technology to solve complicated equations (2) 14%

Use synthetic division to find the roots of an equation (2) 14%

Develop and use properties of matrices (2) 14%

Find the determinant of a matrix (2) 14%

Solve systems of linear inequalities (2) 14%

Relate different representations of lines, curves, and conic sections (2) 14%

Define logarithmic function (2) 14%

Convert between logarithmic and exponential equations (2) 14%

Define the sine, cosine, tangent, cosecant, secant, and cotangent (2) 14%

Express angle measure in degrees or radians when given the trigonometric value (2) 14%

Find partial sums of series (1) 7%

Write equations of lines given various information including parallel and perpendicular lines and vertical and horizontal lines (1) 7%

Confirm the solutions to a quadratic numerically and graphically (1) 7%

Apply quadratics to practical problems (1) 7%

Value of a function for a given domain element (1) 7%

Explore families of functions and recognize and graph various functions: Algebraic (1) 7%

Explore families of functions and recognize and graph various functions: Trigonometric (1) 7%

Investigate functions with a graphing calculator (1) 7%

Solve problems involving direct, inverse, and joint variation (1) 7%

Perform basic operations on polynomials (1) 7%

Perform basic operations on rational expressions (1) 7%

Simplify complex fractions (1) 7%

Inverse of a function and its reflection over $y = x$ (1) 7%

Define the components of a matrix (1) 7%

Find the dimensions of a matrix (1) 7%

Graph rational functions and identify x- and y-intercepts, horizontal asymptotes, and vertical asymptotes (1) 7%

Understand and use fractional exponents (1) 7%

Use the conic sections (1) 7%

Use the defining of logarithms to convert between bases (1) 7%

Geometry

Represent transformations of objects in the plane using coordinates, vectors, functional notation, and matrices (3) 21%

Solve problem involving 2- and 3-dimensional figures using coordinate geometry (2) 14%

Use right triangle trigonometry (2) 14%

Data Analysis

Use technology to analyze functions (3) 21%

Explore questions of experimental design, use of control groups, and reliability (2) 14%

Perform a quadratic regression and use the results (2) 14%

Select appropriate representations and statistics for data (2) 14%

Describe potentially misleading interpretations of data (2) 14%

Describe trends in data and use them to interpret data (2) 14%

Identify how outliers affect representations (1) 7%

Identify purpose of investigation or experiment by stating hypotheses or posing questions (1) 7%

Create a survey instrument where the sample population is identified and the sampling method is specified (1) 7%

Study normal distributions and properties (1) 7%

Analyze the meaning of the maximum or minimum and intercepts of the regression equation as related to bivariate data (1) 7%

Probability

Identify the difference in a permutation and a combination (2) 14%

Design simulations including Monte Carlo simulations to estimate probability (2) 14%

Reasoning

Decide whether a solution is reasonable (2) 14%

Use the properties of number systems and the order of operations to justify the steps in simplifying expressions and solving equations (2) 14%

Decide if an algebraic statement is always, sometimes, or never true (1) 7%

Justify conclusions by deductive and inductive reasoning (1) 7%

Justifies predictions, inferences, or conclusions (1) 7%

Precalculus Standards with Less Agreement
Comparison of Precalculus Course Standards
The set of precalculus course standards for which at most 2 of the 11 states agreed follows:

Sequences
> Perform polynomial division (2) 18%
> Use the rational root theorem (2) 18%
> Work with partial fractions (1) 9%
> Solve quadratic equations with complex coefficients (1) 9%
> Solve rational equations (1) 9%

Functions
> Graph absolute value functions (2) 18%
> Identify 1-to-1, constant, and recursively defined functions (2) 18%
> Define *e* using limit forms (2) 18%
> Perform operations on functions (2) 18%
> Apply circle, angle, and special right triangle relationships (2) 18%
> Develop graphs and apply the six trigonometric functions (2) 18%
> Discuss periodic behavior (2) 18%
> Determine amplitude, period, phase shift, domain, and range of trig functions (2) 18%
> Solve systems of equations, linear and nonlinear (2) 18%
> Calculate determinants of matrices (2) 18%
> Represent vectors graphically and symbolically (2) 18%
> Solve systems of *n* equations (2) 18%
> Apply the fundamental theorem of algebra (2) 18%
> Translate among parametric, algebraic, and geometric representations (2) 18%
> Prove DeMoivre's theorem (2) 18%
> Apply trigonometry and geometry to solve problems (2) 18%
> Use circular functions (1) 9%
> Compute with matrices (1) 9%
> Investigate optimization problems (1) 9%
> Apply successive approximation techniques to determine area (1) 9%

Data Analysis
> Apply binomial, normal, and uniform distributions (2) 18%
> Compare types of errors (1) 9%
> Investigate hypothesis testing (1) 9%
> Model experimental design (1) 9%
> Understand the median fit and least squares regression methods and apply them (1) 9%
> Relate sample statistics to population (1) 9%
> Design surveys (1) 9%

Probability
> Pascal's triangle (2) 18%
> Explain the relationship between theoretical and experimental probability (1) 9%
> Calculate probability of compound events (1) 9%
> Find sample spaces and probability distributions (1) 9%
> Calculate the expected value of random variables (1) 9%
> Apply the counting principle, including combinations and permutations (1) 9%
> Create simulations and experiments and correlate to theoretical probability (1) 9%

Know the definition of independent events (1) 9%
Know and use conditional probabilities (1) 9%

Grades 9–12 (Graduation Standards) with Less Agreement

The set of Grades 9–12, or graduation, standards for which less than 25 percent of the 21 states agreed follows:

Number

Use proportional reasoning to model and solve real-life problems involving direct and inverse variation (5) 24%

Compare subsets of the real number system with regard to their properties: Associative (5) 24%

Compare subsets of the real number system with regard to their properties: Distributive (5) 24%

Apply ratios and proportions to solve problems (5) 24%

Develop fluency with operations (5) 24%

Solve problems using complex numbers (5) 24%

Use a variety of representations to demonstrate an understanding of very large and very small numbers (4) 19%

Compare subsets of the real number system with regard to their properties (4) 19%

Compare subsets of the real number system with regard to their properties: Inverse (4) 19%

Compare subsets of the real number system with regard to their properties: Closure (4) 19%

Use field properties to justify mathematical procedures (4) 19%

Explain the effects of operation on the magnitude of quantities (3) 14%

Estimate the solutions for problem situations involving square and cube roots (3) 14%

Compare subsets of the real number system with regard to their properties: Identity (3) 14%

Solve problem using exponents and logarithms (2) 10%

Explain that vectors and matrices have some properties of real numbers (2) 10%

Identify whether a given set is finite or infinite (1) 5%

Connect physical, verbal, and symbolic representations of irrational numbers (1) 5%

Use factorial notation (1) 5%

Apply factors and greatest common factor (1) 5%

Apply multiples and least common multiple (1) 5%

Apply prime numbers and prime factorization (1) 5%

Describe the relationship between exponential and logarithmic equations (1) 5%

Add in a different base system (1) 5%

Use infinity correctly (1) 5%

Measurement

Convert between the U.S. system and the metric system (5) 24%

Check measurement computations using unit analysis (5) 24%

Solve problems involving unit conversion (4) 19%

Use unit analysis to solve problems involving rates (4) 19%

Determine the measures of central and inscribed angles and their associated arcs (4) 19%

Use significant digits in computational problems (3) 14%

Convert units within the same measurement system (3) 14%

Explain how a small error may lead to a large error in calculated results (2) 10%

Convert angle measures between degrees and radians (2) 10%

Apply concepts of successive approximation (1) 5%

Explain the difference in absolute error and relative error (1) 5%

Algebra

Evaluate polynomial expression for given values of the variable (5) 24%

Describe and compare characteristics of the families of functions (5) 24%

Describe and compare characteristics of the following families of functions: Linear (5) 24%

Describe how a change in the value of a constant or coefficient in a quadratic equation affects the related graphs (5) 24%

Describe and use algebraic manipulations including inverse of functions and compositions of functions (5) 24%

Identify, graph, and describe graphs of basic families of functions: Exponential (5) 24%

Describe slope of a line as a constant rate of change (5) 24%

Identify and use arithmetic and geometric sequences (5) 24%

Compare linear functions algebraically in terms of their rates of change and intercepts (4) 19%

Describe and compare characteristics of the following families of functions: Quadratic (4) 19%

Describe and compare characteristics of the following families of functions: Exponential (4) 19%

Write the equation of a line given 2 points (4) 19%

Generalize patterns using explicitly or recursively defined functions (4) 19%

Use symbolic algebra to represent and solve problems that involve exponential and logarithmic relationships (4) 19%

Solve equations for a specific variable (4) 19%

Create a line of best fit (4) 19%

Use mathematical reasoning to justify conclusions (4) 19%

Find linear equations that represent lines parallel or perpendicular to a given line through a specific point (3) 14%

Describe the effects of parameter changes on exponential functions (3) 14%

Operations on matrices (3) 14%

Demonstrate the relationship among zeros of a function, roots of equations, and solutions of equations (2) 10%

Simplify rational expressions (2) 10%

Use and solve systems of linear and quadratic equations or inequalities with two variables (2) 10%

Identify slope in an equation (2) 10%

Generalize patterns using explicitly designed and recursively defined sequences (2) 10%

Know and use formal notation for sequences and series to solve related problems (2) 10%

Analyze functions and their graphs for symmetries (2) 10%

Apply the laws of exponents to perform operations on expressions (2) 10%

Solve problems with linear programming (2) 10%

Solve equations with square roots (2) 10%

Distinguish between constant and nonconstant (2) 10%

Use formulas to solve problems involving exponential growth and decay (1) 5%

Geometry

Constructions with a straight edge and compass (5) 24%

Prove the Pythagorean theorem (5) 24%

Make conjectures and solve problems involving 2-dimensional objects represented with Cartesian coordinates (5) 24%

Classify angle relationships for parallel lines cut by a transversal (5) 24%

Solve applied problems using triangles (5) 24%

Draw representations of 3-dimensional geometric objects from different perspectives (4) 19%

Identify congruent and similar figures using Euclidean and coordinate geometries (4) 19%

Use and apply matrices to represent translations, reflections, rotations, and dilations (3) 14%

Solve problems using analytic geometry (3) 14%

Law of sines and cosines (3) 14%

Use special right triangles (3) 14%

Cross sections of 3-dimensional objects (3) 14%

Explain slope as a representation of rate of change (2) 10%

Perform simple transformations and their compositions on linear quadratic, logarithmic, and exponential functions (2) 10%

Draw or use visual models to solve problems (2) 10%

Solve problems involving inscribed and circumscribed polygons (2) 10%

Design a net that will create a given figure (2) 10%

Represent transformations of an object in the plane using function notation (2) 10%

Identify conic sections (2) 10%

Determine the relationships among number of vertices, sides, the number of diagonals, and the sum of the angles of a polygon (1) 5%

Rotate conic sections using trigonometric functions (1) 5%

Graph trigonometric functions (1) 5%

Know the six trigonometric functions (1) 5%

Know and use trigonometric inverses (1) 5%

Know the meaning of the terms *frequency, amplitude, phase shift*, and *period* (1) 5%

Data Analysis

Describe and compare various types of studies and identify possible misuses of statistical data (5) 24%

Create and interpret vertex-edge graphs (5) 24%

Apply the multiplication rule of counting (5) 24%

Analyze data using normal distribution (5) 24%

Effect of sample size (5) 24%

Describe measures of center and range of data sets (5) 24%

Use sampling distributions as the basis for inference (5) 24%

Determine if scatter-plot relationship is linear or nonlinear (4) 19%

Analyze and interpret distributions based on spread, symmetry, skewness, clusters, and outliers (4) 19%

Recognize the difference between correlation and causation (4) 19%

Compute and interpret the expected value of random variables (4) 19%

Identify trends in data and support conclusions by using distribution characteristics such as patterns, clusters, and outliers (3) 14%

Identify outliers on a data display (3) 14%

Classify data as univariate or bivariate and as quantitative or qualitative (2) 10%

Law of large numbers (2) 10%

Describe the characteristics of well-designed studies including he role of randomization (2) 10%

Distinguish between a parameter and a statistic (2) 10%

Use simulations to describe the variability of sample statistics from a known population (1) 5%

Display bivariate data where at least one variable is categorical (1) 5%

Describe difference among studies, recognizing when inference can be drawn (1) 5%

Describe how sample statistics reflect the vales of population parameters (1) 5%

Understand the central limit theorem (1) 5%

Probability

Use and describe how to compute the probability of a compound event (5) 24%

Determine theoretical probability for a chance event (5) 24%

Explain the relationship between the probability of an event occurring and the odds of an event occurring and compute one given the other (4) 19%

Determine geometric probability (4) 19%

Follow and interpret processes expressed in flow charts (1) 5%

Describe the normal curve and use its properties (1) 5%

Create and interpret a probability distribution (1) 5%

Probability and Statistics Course Standards with Less Agreement

The standards listed below are those that were listed by only 1 of the 6 states.

Statistics

Organize and describe distributions of data by using frequency tables

Organize and describe distributions of data by using standard line graph

Organize and describe distributions of data by using standard bar graph

Examine graphs of data for clusters and gaps

Analyze kurtosis and skewness in conjunction with other descriptive measures

Describe errors inherent in extrapolation

Produce a two-way table as a summary of two categorical variables

Calculate marginal, relative, and conditional frequencies in a two-way table

Use marginal, relative and conditional frequencies to analyze data

Compare population and sample and parameter and statistic

Identify possible sources of bias in a survey

Probability

Calculate geometric probability

Create simulations and experiments that correlate to theoretical probability

Apply the concept of a random variable to generate and interpret probability distributions

Calculate relative frequency and expected frequency

Compare Type I and Type II errors

Identify the properties of a t-distribution

Compare a t-distribution and a normal distribution